Bake & Enjoy

Published by Brolga Publishing Pty Ltd
ABN 46 063 962 443
PO Box 452
Torquay Victoria 3228
Australia

email: markzocchi@brolgapublishing.com.au

National Library of Australia
Cataloguing-in-Publication data
Rachel Gray, author.
ISBN 9780909608798 (paperback)

A catalogue record for this book is available from the National Library of Australia

Printed in Malaysia
Cover design and Typesetting by Elly Cridland

Bake & Enjoy

Rachel Gray

This book is affectionately dedicated to my mum for inspiring my passion for baking.

- CONTENTS -

INTRODUCTION

My earliest memories in the kitchen are of making icing for cupcakes and whipping cream. These tasks were always completed with mum by my side reminding me not to add too much food colouring or overbeat the cream and turn it to butter. As she would say, "You can always add but you can't take away". This was the first of many lessons my mother taught me about baking and she has greatly inspired my passion. Like her, I find joy in making delicious food to share with my friends and family.

Mum is an outstanding country-style home baker well renowned within her community for her skill. Her cakes are sought out at cake stalls, people come knocking on her door to ask for a bottle of her relish and she has won hundreds of prizes for her baking entries in the local show. She began cooking when she was 12, whisking eggs and sugar for a sponge cake using rotary beaters and baking them in a wood fired stove. The smell of cake for the shearers, jam to use up an abundance of fruit or scones to welcome guests has been emanating from her kitchen ever since.

Mum recalls her recipes from memory and measures out the ingredients with an old tea cup and an experienced eye. Any of her recipes that are written down include imperial or imprecise measurements such as 'a small cup of sugar' and minimal instructions. This prompted me to compile her recipes so I could easily access them and competently replicate her baking. I also wanted to preserve her treasured recipes so they could be shared with her other children and grandchildren.

I began by transcribing Mum's recipes with standard measuring cups and detailed instructions and gathering all of her baking tips and tricks. I then converted the recipes so they could be made successfully and quickly in the Thermomix. The book expanded over time as I began experimenting with the basic recipes to include the flavours and ingredients my husband and children enjoy. I also saw the importance of adapting the recipes to be gluten-free and vegan friendly considering today's prominence of food allergies and dietary restrictions.

In the process I discovered how much I enjoy baking. I find the process and the aroma that fills the house therapeutic and I feel a great sense of accomplishment as I master a new recipe. I love the way that sharing delicious, home baked food sends warm messages and brings a smile to the faces of my family and friends. It's an activity my children and I enjoy doing together and I'm proud to be able to pass on to them the skills my mother taught me.

Baking is a skill that has been valued in my family and I am grateful to have. I know there are many people out there who don't bake because they believe they can't, they don't have the time or they think that allergy friendly food doesn't taste good. These recipes don't require any extraordinary baking skills or exuberant amounts of time yet they never fail to please. Here is my collection of updated classic treats to fill up the biscuit jar, pop in the lunch box or celebrate a birthday. I hope that they will inspire even the most reluctant of bakers to put on an apron and bake something delicious to enjoy with their family and friends. Happy Baking!

CAKES

HOW TO BAKE BUTTER CAKES

PREPARE THE CAKE TIN

It's tempting to skip over this step because most cake tins available today are non-stick, however it is more annoying to turn out your cake and discover half of it is stuck inside the tin. I find that greasing the base and sides of the tin then just lining the base is enough to ensure the cakes come out cleanly.

Grease the tin with a cold cube of butter or baking spray. Trace around the base of the tin on baking paper and cut just inside the pencil mark. Place the paper inside the tin then rub to stick it to the base and remove any air bubbles.

MIX THE BATTER

Traditionally butter cakes are made by creaming the butter and sugar, beating in the eggs one at a time then folding through the dry ingredients alternately with the liquids. This isn't hard but it does take a little more time. For most of my butter cakes, I place all of the ingredients into a bowl then beat with a paddle attachment on medium speed for a couple of minutes just until the batter is smooth.

The only trick to this method is to make sure the butter is very soft so it combines easily with the other ingredients without excessive beating. To soften butter, cut it into cubes and leave it at room temperature or microwave briefly on defrost. You can also beat it for 40 to 60 seconds at 37°C, Speed 4 in the Thermomix. The butter shouldn't give any resistance when pushed but it shouldn't be melted.

FILL THE CAKE TIN

Pour the batter into the tin then use a spatula to spread the mixture evenly. The mixture shouldn't fill more than 2⁄3 of the tin to allow room for the cake to rise. Give the pan a little shake to eradicate any air bubbles then the batter is ready to bake.

BAKE

Turning on the oven to preheat is always the first step but check to make sure the oven has reached the correct temperature before you put the cake in. Place the cake in the centre of the oven where the air can circulate around it so that it bakes evenly. Avoid opening the oven door for a peek until at least ¾ of the cooking time has passed otherwise the cake may sink in the middle. After this time, the cake can be rotated 180° if the top is browning unevenly or covered with foil it is becoming too dark.

TEST FOR DONENESS

To test if the cake is cooked, insert a skewer into the centre. If the skewer comes out clean or with a few cooked cake crumbs clinging to it, the cake is ready. If the skewer has streaks of batter, bake for a further 5 to 10 minutes then test again.

COOL

Cakes are a little delicate straight from the oven so they need to rest in the pan for 10 minutes so they don't crack or crumble. After this short cooling off period, run a knife or a thin spatula around the edge of the tin to release the sides of the cake. Invert it onto a wire rack to cool and cover it with a clean tea towel to trap in moisture. The cake can then be iced once it has completely cooled.

STORE

Store cakes in an airtight container at room temperature unless they have cream fillings or icings in which case they should be refrigerated. To freeze, wrap in plastic then place in an airtight container for up to 2 months.

BASIC BUTTER CAKE
SERVES 12 GFA

250g butter, very well softened
1 cup (220g) sugar
4 eggs
1⅔ cups (250g) self-raising flour
1 teaspoon vanilla extract
¼ cup (60g) milk

Buttercream Icing
250g cold, unsalted butter
3 cups (480g) icing sugar
2 tablespoons (40g) milk
1 teaspoon vanilla extract
Food dye (optional)

Preheat oven to 160°C. Grease and line a 20cm square cake tin or a 23cm round cake tin.
Beat butter, sugar, eggs, flour and vanilla on medium speed for 2 minutes until mixture is creamy and pale.
TM 40 seconds/Speed 4. Scrape halfway.
Add milk then beat until smooth.
TM 20 seconds/Speed 4.
Pour mixture into pan and bake for 40 to 50 minutes or until cooked when tested with a skewer. Stand for 5 minutes then turn out onto a wire rack to cool.

Buttercream Icing
Beat butter on a medium speed until soft and pale.
TM 2 minutes/Speed 3.
Add half of the icing sugar. Beat until fluffy.
TM 3.5 minutes/Speed 3.
Add remaining icing sugar, milk, vanilla and food dye and beat until smooth.
TM Butterfly/1 minute/Speed 3.
Spread icing over top and sides of cake.

DIETARY ALTERATIONS

GF Self-raising flour = 250g GF self-raising flour.
Use 6 eggs.

VARIATIONS

Chocolate Butter Cake
For cake use 1½ cups (225g) of self-raising flour and ¼ cup (25g) of cocoa powder.
For icing use 2 ⅔ cups (430g) of icing sugar and ½ cup (50g) of cocoa.

Neapolitan Cake
Grease 3 x 20cm cake tins.
Prepare a half batch of chocolate cake and 1 quantity of butter cake. Tint half of the butter cake mixture pink. Spread each batter into a separate tin. Bake for 20 to 25 minutes.
Sandwich the chocolate, pink and vanilla layers with Chantilly cream (pg. 171) then ice top and sides of cake with buttercream icing.

Marble Cake
Grease and line a 23cm round cake tin.
Prepare a half batch of chocolate cake and 1 quantity of butter cake. Tint half of the butter cake mixture pink.
Drop spoonfuls of the three mixtures alternatively into tin. Swirl a knife through the batter to create a marbled effect. Bake for 50 minutes to 1 hour.

VANILLA CUPCAKES

MAKES 12 GFA

120g butter, very well softened
120g caster sugar
2 eggs
1½ teaspoons vanilla bean paste
120g self-raising flour
2 tablespoons (25g) cornflour
1½ tablespoons (30g) milk

Vanilla Icing
1½ cups (240g) icing sugar
60g butter
1 tablespoon (20g) milk
1 teaspoon vanilla extract

Preheat oven to 170°C. Line a 12 hole muffin pan with paper cases.
Beat ingredients together on medium speed for 2 minutes until mixture is smooth.
TM 2 minutes/Speed 3. Scrape halfway.
Divide mixture between the paper cases. Bake for 14 to 16 minutes or until cooked when tested with a skewer. Cupcakes will still be quite pale on top.
Transfer to a wire rack to cool.

Vanilla Icing
Beat ingredients together until smooth.
TM 40 seconds/Speed 4. Scrape halfway.
Spread icing over cupcakes.

DIETARY ALTERATIONS

GF Self-raising flour = 120g GF self-raising flour.
Use 3 eggs.

VARIATIONS

Baby Cupcakes
Divide mixture between 36 mini muffin cases. Bake for 11 to 13 minutes.

Butterfly Cupcakes
Cut a shallow circle from the top of each cake. Fill holes with strawberry cream (pg. 171) or lemon curd (pg. 175). Halve cake top and push the pieces into the filling to resemble wings. Dust with icing sugar to serve.

Chocolate Cupcakes
Replace cornflour with ¼ cup (25g) of cocoa powder.
Add 2 tablespoons (20g) cocoa to icing.

VEGAN VANILLA CUPCAKES
MAKES 12 V

125g vegan butter, very well softened
¾ cup (165g) caster sugar
1½ cups (225g) self-raising flour
¼ cup (35g) custard powder
½ teaspoon baking powder
½ cup (125g) soy milk
2 tablespoons (40g) water
2 teaspoon white vinegar
2 teaspoons vanilla extract

Vegan Swiss Meringue Buttercream
90g aquafaba
1/8 teaspoon cream of tartar
340g pure icing sugar
340g vegan butter
2 teaspoons vanilla extract

Preheat oven to 170°C. Line a 12 hole muffin pan with paper cases.
Place all ingredients into the bowl of an electric mixer fitted with a paddle attachment. Beat on medium speed for 2 minutes until mixture is smooth.
TM 2 minutes/Speed 3. Scrape halfway.
Divide mixture between the paper cases. Bake for 17 to 19 minutes or until cooked when tested with a skewer. Transfer to a wire rack to cool.

Vegan Swiss Meringue Buttercream
Place aquafaba, cream of tartar and icing sugar into the bowl of an electric mixer fitted with a whisk attachment. Beat on medium-high speed for 5 minutes or until the sugar has dissolved.
TM Butterfly/5 minutes/Speed 3.
Add half of the butter and continue to beat until thickened. Mixture may appear curdled at this stage.
TM 1 minute/Butterfly/Speed 3.
Add remaining butter and beat until mixture is smooth and thick.
TM 30 seconds/Butterfly/Speed 3.
Beat in vanilla until incorporated.
TM 30 seconds/Speed 3.

VARIATION

Vegan Vanilla Cake
Bake mixture in a 20cm round cake tin for 35 to 40 minutes or until a skewer comes out clean.

MADELEINES
MAKES 18 GFA

100g butter
2 teaspoons (15g) honey
1 teaspoon vanilla bean paste
2 eggs
1/3 cup (75g) sugar
2/3 cup (100g) plain flour
¾ teaspoon baking powder

Preheat oven to 180°C. Grease and flour an 18 hole madeleine pan.
Melt butter then stir in honey and vanilla. Set aside.
Beat eggs and sugar until pale and frothy.
TM Butterfly/3 minutes/37°C/Speed 3.
Sift in flour and baking powder and fold through.
TM Butterfly/10 seconds/Speed 3.
Whisk in the melted butter mixture until just combined.
TM Butterfly/10 seconds/Speed 3.
Pipe or spoon batter into moulds. Bake for 8 to 10 minutes until puffed and golden.
Dust with icing sugar and serve whilst still warm.

DIETARY ALTERATION

GF Plain flour = 75g GF plain flour + 25g cornflour.

VARIATIONS

Orange & Cinnamon Madeleines
Finely grate the rind of 1 orange.
TM 20 seconds/Speed 9. Scrape halfway.
Beat orange zest with eggs and sugar.
To serve, brush cakes with orange juice and sprinkle with 2 tablespoons of caster sugar mixed with ½ teaspoon of cinnamon.

Honey Chai Madeleines
Add 1 teaspoon of mixed spice, ½ teaspoon of ground ginger, and ¼ teaspoon of ground cardamom with flour.
To serve, melt 2 teaspoons (10g) of butter with 2 tablespoons (60g) of honey and brush over cakes.

Lemon Madeleines
Replace honey and vanilla bean paste with 3 teaspoons (15g) of lemon juice.
To serve, mix ¼ cup (40g) of pure icing sugar with 1 tablespoon (20g) of lemon juice.
TM 1 minute/Speed 3
Drizzle over cakes whilst still hot to glaze.

BAKERS NOTES

Madeleines are best eaten warm from the oven. The batter can be prepared in advance then covered and refrigerated for up to 24 hours until ready to bake.

TEA CAKE

SERVES 8 GFA

125g butter, very well softened
¾ cup (165g) caster sugar
2 eggs
2 teaspoons vanilla extract
1½ cups (225g) self-raising flour
½ cup (125g) milk

Preheat oven to 170°C. Grease and line a 20cm round cake tin.
Place all ingredients into the bowl of an electric mixer fitted with a paddle attachment. Beat on medium speed for 2 minutes until mixture is smooth and pale.
TM 2 minutes/Speed 3. Scrape halfway.
Pour mixture into prepared pan. Bake for 35 to 45 minutes or until a skewer comes out clean. Stand for 10 minutes before turning out onto a wire rack. Dust with icing sugar and serve whilst warm.

DIETARY ALTERATIONS

GF Self-raising flour = 225g GF self-raising flour.

VARIATIONS

Raspberry & White Chocolate Tea Cake
Pour batter into a 27 x 17.5cm slice tray.
Sprinkle over 100g of white choc-chips and 125g of raspberries then bake.

Apple & Cinnamon Tea Cake
Peel, core and finely slice a large Granny Smith apple. Arrange slices over cake batter then bake.
Brush hot cake with 1 tablespoon of melted butter and sprinkle over 2 tablespoons of caster sugar mixed with ½ teaspoon of cinnamon.

LEMON & BLUEBERRY CAKE

SERVES 8 GFA VA

Zest of 2 lemons
125g butter, very well softened
¾ cup (165g) caster sugar
2 eggs
1½ cups (225g) self-raising flour
½ teaspoon bicarbonate of soda.
½ cup (120g) sour cream
¼ cup (60g) lemon juice
125g punnet blueberries
2 teaspoons plain flour

Lemon Topping
¼ cup (55g) caster sugar
1½ tablespoons (30g) lemon juice

Preheat oven to 170°C. Grease and line a 23 x 13 cm loaf tin.
Finely grate lemon zest into a large mixing bowl.
TM 20 seconds/Speed 9. Scrape halfway.
Add remaining ingredients except for blueberries and plain flour. Beat on medium speed for 2 minutes until mixture is smooth and pale.
TM 2 minutes/Speed 3. Scrape halfway.
Wash and drain blueberries then toss in plain flour. Spread cake batter in pan then sprinkle over blueberries. Bake for 40 minutes or until a skewer comes out clean.

Lemon Topping
Mix sugar and lemon juice. Spoon topping over hot cake. Rest for 10 minutes then transfer to a wire rack to cool.

DIETARY ALTERATIONS

GF Self-raising flour = 225g GF self-raising flour.
Plain flour = 2 teaspoons GF plain flour.
V Butter = vegan butter.
Eggs = ¼ cup (60g) aquafaba + 2 tablespoons (20g) tapioca flour.
Sour cream = ½ cup (125g) coconut yogurt.

ORANGE CAKE

SERVES 12 GFA VA

2/3 cup (160g) thickened cream
½ cup (125g) orange juice
100ml (90g) mild olive oil
Zest of 2 oranges
4 eggs
1½ cups (330g) caster sugar
1¼ cups (185g) plain flour
1¼ cups (125g) almond meal
2 teaspoons baking powder
Icing sugar for dusting

Preheat oven to 160°C. Grease and line the base of a 25cm round springform tin.
Measure cream, orange juice and olive oil into a jug. Set aside.
Finely grate orange zest into a large mixing bowl.
TM 20 seconds/Speed 9. Scrape halfway.
Add eggs and sugar then beat until pale and fluffy.
TM Butterfly/4 minutes/37°C/Speed 4/ MC off.
Gradually add olive oil mixture and beat to combine.
TM Butterfly/1 minute/Speed 2. Add gradually.
Fold through flour, almond meal and baking powder.
TM Butterfly/10 seconds/Speed 4.
Pour mixture into tin. Bake for 40 to 50 minutes until cooked when tested with a skewer. Stand for 10 minutes before turning out to cool.
Dust with icing sugar to serve.

DIETARY ALTERATIONS

GF Plain flour = 100g GF plain flour + 100g buckwheat flour.
V Thickened cream = 2⁄3 cup (165g) coconut yogurt.
Eggs = ½ cup (125g) aquafaba + 2 tablespoons (20g) tapioca flour.

SULTANA CAKE

SERVES 12 GFA

1¼ cups (250g) sultanas
¼ cup (60g) water
2 tablespoons (40g) lemon juice
Zest of 1 lemon
125g butter, very well softened
½ cup (110g) sugar
2 eggs
125g plain flour, plus 2 teaspoons extra
½ teaspoon baking powder

Place sultanas, water and lemon juice into a saucepan and bring to the boil. Boil gently for 5 to 10 minutes or until liquid has been absorbed. Set aside to cool.
TM 10 minutes/100°C/Reverse/Soft Stir. Set aside.
Preheat oven to 140°C. Grease and line a 10cm x 20cm loaf tin with baking paper.
Finely grate lemon zest into a mixing bowl.
TM 20 seconds/Speed 9. Scrape halfway.
Add butter, sugar, eggs, 125g of flour and baking powder. Beat on medium speed for 2 minutes until mixture is smooth and pale.
TM 2 minutes/Speed 3. Scrape halfway.
Add extra flour to sultanas and stir to coat. Fold sultanas through cake batter until evenly distributed.
TM 10 seconds/Reverse/Speed 3.
Spread the mixture into pan. Bake for 60 to 75 minutes until a skewer comes out clean. Remove cake from tin and wrap in foil. Allow to cool overnight before slicing.

DIETARY ALTERATIONS

GF Plain flour = 90g GF plain flour + 35g besan flour.
Coat sultanas in in extra 2 teaspoons of GF flour.

CARAMEL SOUR CREAM CAKE
SERVES 12 GFA VA

180g butter, very well softened
1¼ cups (275g) brown sugar
3 eggs
1½ tablespoons (45g) golden syrup
1½ teaspoons vanilla bean paste
2 cups (300g) self-raising flour
¾ cup (180g) sour cream

Caramelised Nuts
½ cup (40g) flaked almonds
2 teaspoons maple syrup

Caramel Cream Cheese
150g cream cheese
100g salted butter
⅔ cup (145g) brown sugar
1 tablespoon (30g) golden syrup
1 teaspoon vanilla bean paste

Preheat oven to 170°C. Grease and line 2 x 20cm round cake tins.
Place all ingredients into the bowl of an electric mixer fitted with a paddle attachment. Beat on medium speed for 2 minutes until mixture is smooth and pale.
TM 2 minutes/Speed 3. Scrape halfway.
Divide batter between pans. Bake for 25 to 30 minutes until a skewer comes out clean. Rest for 10 minutes then turn out onto a wire rack to cool.

Caramelised Nuts
Mix almonds with maple syrup then spread over a lined oven tray. Bake for 5 to 10 minutes until golden.

Caramel Cream Cheese
Beat ingredients together on medium speed until smooth.
TM 1 minute/Speed 4. Scrape halfway.
Use icing to sandwich cake layers then spread remaining icing over the top and sides of the cake. Sprinkle with caramelised nuts to decorate.

DIETARY ALTERATIONS
GF SR flour = 300g GF self-raising flour.
V Butter = vegan butter.
Eggs = 90ml aquafaba + ¼ cup (35g) tapioca flour.
Sour cream = ¾ cup (185g) coconut yogurt.
Cream cheese = Extra 150g vegan butter + 2 teaspoons apple cider vinegar.

VARIATIONS

Coffee Cake
Dissolve 1½ tablespoons of instant coffee in 1 tablespoon of boiling water and add to cake batter. Use walnuts in place of almonds.

Ginger Cake
Add 3 teaspoons of ground ginger, 1½ teaspoons of mixed spice and ½ cup (100g) sliced glacé ginger to batter. Bake in 2 x 10cm x 20cm loaf tins. Drizzle with lemon glacé icing (pg. 170).

RED VELVET CAKE
SERVES 12 GFA

150g butter, very well softened
1/3 cup (70g) mild olive oil
1½ cups (330g) caster sugar
3 eggs
2 teaspoons vanilla extract
2 cups (300g) self-raising flour
¼ cup (25g) cocoa
¾ cup (180g) buttermilk
1 teaspoon red gel food dye
¾ teaspoon white vinegar

Cream Cheese Icing
250g butter
250g cream cheese
3 cups (480g) icing sugar

Preheat oven to 160°C. Grease and line 2 x 20cm round tins.
Place all ingredients into the bowl of an electric mixer fitted with a paddle attachment. Beat on medium speed for 2 minutes until mixture is smooth and pale.
TM 2 minutes/Speed 3. Scrape halfway.
Divide batter between pans. Bake for 30 to 35 minutes or until a skewer comes out clean. Rest for 10 minutes then turn out onto a wire rack to cool.

Cream Cheese Icing
Beat butter and cream cheese on medium speed until pale and smooth.
TM 3 minutes/Speed 3. Scrape halfway.
Add icing sugar and beat until mixture is creamy and fluffy.
TM Butterfly/1 minute/Speed 3.
Use cream cheese icing to sandwich cake layers then spread remaining icing over the top and sides of the cake.

DIETARY ALTERATION
GF Self-raising flour = 300g GF self-raising flour.

VEGAN RED VELVET CAKE
SERVES 12 V

¾ cup (185g) soy milk
3 teaspoons white vinegar
1 tablespoon psyllium husk
150g vegan butter, very well softened
⅓ cup (70g) mild olive oil
1½ cups (330g) caster sugar
90ml (90g) aquafaba
2 teaspoons vanilla extract
2 cups (300g) self-raising flour
¼ cup (25g) cocoa
1 teaspoon red gel food dye

Cream Cheese Icing
180g vegan butter
3½ cups (560g) icing sugar
2 tablespoons (40g) soy milk
2 teaspoons apple cider vinegar
1 teaspoon vanilla extract

Preheat oven to 160°C. Grease and line 2 x 20cm round tins.
Place milk, vinegar and psyllium husk into the bowl of an electric mixer. Stir then allow to stand for 5 minutes.
Add remaining ingredients. Beat on medium speed using a paddle attachment for 2 minutes until smooth.
TM 2 minutes/Speed 3. Scrape halfway.
Divide batter between pans. Bake for 30 to 35 minutes or until a skewer comes out clean. Rest in tin for 20 minutes then turn out onto a wire rack to cool.

Cream Cheese Icing
Beat ingredients together until smooth.
TM 20 seconds/Speed 4.
Use cream cheese icing to sandwich cake layers then spread remaining icing over the top and sides of the cake.

CHOCOLATE BUTTERMILK CAKE

SERVES 12 GFA

125g butter, very well softened
2/3 cup (145g) caster sugar
1/2 cup (110g) dark brown sugar
2 eggs
1 teaspoon vanilla extract
1 1/2 cups (225g) self-raising flour
1/2 cup (50g) cocoa powder
1/2 teaspoon bicarbonate of soda
1 cup (240g) buttermilk

Chocolate Icing
1 1/2 cups (240g) icing sugar
60g butter
2 tablespoons (20g) cocoa
2 tablespoons (40g) milk

Preheat oven to 160°C. Grease and line a 20cm square cake tin.
Place all ingredients into the bowl of an electric mixer fitted with a paddle attachment. Beat on medium speed for 2 minutes until mixture is smooth and pale.
TM 2 minutes/Speed 3. Scrape halfway.
Pour mixture into pan. Bake for 45 to 55 minutes or until a skewer comes out clean. Stand for 10 minutes then turn onto a wire rack to cool before icing.

Chocolate Icing
Beat ingredients together until smooth.
TM 40 seconds/Speed 4. Scrape halfway.
Spread icing over the top of cake.

DIETARY ALTERATION

GF Self raising flour = 225g GF self-raising flour.
Use 3 eggs.
Bake for 40 to 50 minutes.

VEGAN CHOCOLATE CAKE

SERVES 12 V

1 cup (250g) soy milk
1 tablespoon (20ml) apple cider vinegar
125g vegan butter, very well softened
2/3 cup (145g) caster sugar
1/2 cup (110g) dark brown sugar
1/4 cup (60g) aquafaba
1 teaspoon vanilla extract
1 1/2 cups (225g) self-raising flour
1/2 cup (50g) cocoa powder
1/2 teaspoon bicarbonate of soda

Chocolate Icing
1 1/2 cups (240g) icing sugar
60g vegan butter
2 tablespoons (20g) cocoa
1 1/2 tablespoons (30g) soy milk

Preheat oven to 160°C. Grease a 20cm square cake tin and line base with baking paper.
Mix milk with vinegar in the bowl of an electric mixer. Allow to stand for 5 minutes. Add remaining ingredients. Beat on medium speed using a paddle attachment for 2 minutes until smooth.
TM 2 minutes/Speed 3. Scrape halfway.
Pour mixture into pan. Bake for 45 to 55 minutes or until a skewer comes out clean. Rest in tin for 20 minutes then turn out onto a wire rack to cool.

Chocolate Icing
Beat ingredients together until smooth.
TM 40 seconds/Speed 4. Scrape halfway.
Spread icing over the top of cake.

ALMOND CAKE
SERVES 12 GFA VA

200g butter
1 cup (220g) sugar
4 eggs
1½ teaspoons vanilla extract
2 cups (200g) almond meal
⅓ cup (50g) self-raising flour
¼ cup (30g) flaked almonds

Preheat oven to 160°C. Grease a 25cm round, springform cake tin and line base with baking paper.
Beat butter and sugar on low speed until combined.
TM 2 minutes/Speed 3.
Increase speed to medium and beat until pale and creamy.
TM 1 minute/Speed 4.
Add eggs and vanilla then beat until incorporated.
TM 20 seconds/Speed 4. Scrape halfway.
Fold through almond meal and flour.
TM 20 seconds/Speed 3. Scrape halfway.
Pour the mixture into tin. Sprinkle over flaked almonds. Bake for 45 to 60 minutes until golden and a skewer comes out clean. If the cake is becoming too dark whilst baking, cover the top with foil until cooked through. Allow cake to cool completely in tin.

DIETARY ALTERATIONS

GF Self-raising flour = 50g GF self-raising flour.
V Butter = vegan butter.
Eggs = ½ cup (125g) aquafaba + ¼ cup (30g) tapioca flour.

VARIATIONS

Raspberry, Coconut & Almond Cake
Replace flour with ¾ cup (60g) desiccated coconut. Spread mixture into pan. Sprinkle over 150g of raspberries and ¼ cup of flaked almonds.
Bake then dust with icing sugar to serve.

Chocolate & Hazelnut Cake
Substitute self-raising flour with ½ cup (50g) of cocoa powder and use hazelnut meal instead of almond meal. Glaze with chocolate ganache (page 173).

RHUBARB CRUMBLE CAKE

SERVES 12 GFA VA

Topping
¾ cup (90g) pecans
¼ cup (55g) sugar

Cake Batter
1¼ cups (275g) brown sugar
125g unsalted butter
2 eggs
1 teaspoon vanilla bean paste
1 cup (240g) buttermilk
2¼ cups (340g) plain flour
1 teaspoon bicarbonate of soda
1½ teaspoons ground ginger
½ teaspoon salt
2 cups rhubarb cut into 1cm slices
1 teaspoon finely grated orange zest

Topping
Finely chop pecans and place in a small bowl.
TM 3 seconds/Speed 6. Set aside.
Stir in sugar.

Cake Batter
Preheat oven to 170°C. Grease and line a 20cm square cake tin allowing paper to extend above the rim of the tin.
Cream butter and sugar until pale and fluffy.
TM 2 minutes/Speed 4. Scrape halfway.
Beat in eggs, vanilla and buttermilk.
TM 20 seconds/Speed 4.
Sift in flour, bicarbonate of soda, ginger and salt and mix until smooth.
TM 20 seconds/Speed 4. Scrape halfway
Stir rhubarb and orange zest through the batter.
TM 10 seconds/Reverse/Speed 4. Assist with spatula.
Spread the mixture into the tin then sprinkle with topping. Bake for 1 hour or until a skewer comes out clean.
Allow cake to cool in tin for 10 minutes. Use the baking paper to lift the cake out of the tin and onto a wire rack to cool.

DIETARY ALTERATIONS

GF Plain flour = 200g GF plain flour + 140g buckwheat flour.
V Butter = vegan butter.
Eggs = ¼ cup (60g) aquafaba + 1 tablespoon (10g) tapioca flour.
Buttermilk = ½ cup (125g) coconut yogurt + ½ cup (125g) soy milk

VARIATION

Apple Crumble Cake
Exchange rhubarb for peeled and diced apple and ground ginger for mixed spice. Omit orange zest.

BANANA CAKE
SERVES 12 GFA

1 cup (250g) peeled, overripe bananas
125g butter, very well softened
1 cup (220g) caster sugar
2 eggs
2 teaspoons vanilla extract
1½ cups (225g) self-raising flour
½ teaspoon bicarbonate of soda
½ cup (120g) buttermilk

Caramel Glaze
125g butter
½ cup (120g) thickened cream
½ cup (110g) brown sugar
1 teaspoon vanilla bean paste
¾ cup (120g) icing sugar

Preheat oven to 160°C. Grease a 22cm Bundt tin.
Mash bananas in a large mixing bowl.
TM 5 seconds/Speed 5.
Add remaining ingredients. Beat on medium speed for 2 minutes or until mixture is smooth and pale.
TM 3 minutes/Speed 3. Scrape halfway.
Pour mixture into tin. Bake for 30 to 40 minutes until a skewer comes out clean. Stand for 5 minutes then turn onto a wire rack to cool completely.

Caramel Glaze
Melt butter with cream, brown sugar, and vanilla in a saucepan over medium heat. Bring to the boil stirring for 5 minutes or until sauce coats the back of a spoon.
TM 8 minutes/Varoma/Speed 2/MC off.
Sift in icing sugar and whisk well to combine.
TM 20 seconds/Speed 4.
Allow to cool slightly before pouring over cake.

DIETARY ALTERATION
GF Self-raising flour = 225g GF self-raising flour.

VEGAN BANANA CAKE
SERVES 12 V

½ cup (125g) soy milk
1 tablespoon (20ml) apple cider vinegar
1 cup (250g) peeled, overripe bananas
125g vegan butter, well softened
1 cup (220g) caster sugar
1 teaspoon vanilla extract
1½ cups (225g) self-raising flour
1 teaspoon bicarbonate of soda

Caramel Glaze
1 x 320g tin sweetened condensed coconut milk
2 tablespoons (60g) golden syrup
50g vegan butter

Preheat oven to 160°C. Grease a 22cm Bundt tin.
Mix soy milk with apple cider vinegar. Allow to stand for 10 minutes.
Mash bananas in a large mixing bowl.
TM 5 seconds/Speed 5.
Add milk and remaining ingredients to mashed banana. Beat on medium speed for 2 minutes or until mixture is smooth and pale.
TM 3 minutes/Speed 3. Scrape halfway.
Pour mixture into tin. Bake for 35 to 40 minutes until a skewer comes out clean. Cool for 5 minutes then turn onto a wire rack to cool completely.

Caramel Glaze
Place all ingredients into a saucepan over a medium heat. Bring to the boil, stirring, then remove from heat.
TM 7 minutes/Varoma/Speed 2.
Allow to cool slightly before pouring over cake.

CARROT CAKE
SERVES 12 GFA VA

1 cup (100g) walnuts
500g carrots, peeled
1¾ cups (385g) sugar
1¼ cups (280g) mild olive oil
4 eggs
1 teaspoon vanilla essence
2 cups (300g) plain flour
2 teaspoons bicarbonate of soda
2 teaspoons cinnamon
2 teaspoons mixed spice
½ teaspoon salt
Toasted walnuts and pumpkin seeds to decorate

Cream Cheese Icing
250g butter
250g cream cheese
3 cups (480g) icing sugar

Preheat oven to 170°C. Grease and line 2 x 20cm round cake tins.
Chop walnuts then set aside.
TM 1 second/Speed 5. Set aside.
Grate carrots then set aside with walnuts.
TM 5 seconds/Speed 5. Set aside.
Place sugar, olive oil, eggs and vanilla into a large mixing bowl. Beat until well combined.
TM 20 seconds/Speed 4.
Sift in flour, bicarbonate of soda, cinnamon, mixed spice and salt. Stir until well combined.
TM 20 seconds/Speed 4. Scrape halfway.
Fold through walnuts and carrot.
TM 10 seconds/Reverse/Speed 4.
Divide mixture between tins. Bake for 55 to 60 minutes or until a skewer comes out clean. Stand in tins for 10 minutes then turn out onto a wire rack to cool completely.

Cream Cheese Icing
Beat butter on medium speed until pale and smooth.
TM 2 minutes/Speed 3. Scrape halfway.
Add cream cheese and half of the icing sugar. Beat until well combined.
TM 2 minutes/Speed 3.
Add remaining icing sugar. Beat until mixture is creamy and fluffy.
TM Butterfly/1 minute/Speed 3.
Use cream cheese icing to sandwich cake layers then spread remaining icing over the top and sides of the cake. Sprinkle over walnuts and pumpkin seeds to decorate.

DIETARY ALTERATIONS

GF Plain flour = 150g GF plain flour + 150g buckwheat flour.
V Eggs = 125ml water + ¼ cup (30g) tapioca flour + 1 tablespoon apple cider vinegar.
Ice with vegan cream cheese (pg. 171)

SPONGE CAKES

HOW TO BAKE FEATHERLIGHT SPONGE CAKES

PREPARE THE CAKE TIN

If you want to bake an impressive double sponge cake, you need to grease and flour the tins. This allows the cakes to cling to sides of the pan so they rise then helps them to release from the tins. For rolled sponge cakes, lightly grease the tin with a cold cube of butter then line with a sheet of baking paper.

BEAT THE EGGS AND SUGAR

Bigger is better when it comes to choosing eggs for a sponge cake. I upsize my eggs and use jumbo eggs from a 800g carton. Make sure they are fresh and at room temperature for maximum aeration. I grew up gradually adding the sugar a spoonful at a time to the eggs but have discovered that I can achieve the same result with less effort. Instead, beat the eggs and sugar together on high speed using a whisk attachment for around 15 minutes. After this time the mixture should be very thick and pale and should have tripled in volume.

SIFT THE DRY INGREDIENTS

Sifting is a necessity for sponge cakes even when using the Thermomix. It ensures the dry ingredients are evenly mixed and helps them to fold easily into the eggs. Sift onto sheets of baking paper so you can pour the flour mixture back into the sifter or into the bowl without a mess.

FOLD IN THE FLOUR

This step sounds a little daunting but in reality it isn't that hard. The flour needs to be folded in gently but quickly to avoid deflating the beaten eggs. To fold in the flour, make a ferris wheel motion with a metal whisk, turning the bowl 90° after every few turns.

ADD THE LIQUIDS

Mix the liquids and have them ready to be added as soon as the flour has been folded in. Pour the liquids around the side of the bowl then fold through using a thin spatula.
Make sure the flour is fully incorporated at this stage because any clumps of flour won't dissipate during cooking. When using the Thermomix, remove the butterfly and tap it gently on the side of the bowl to dislodge any flour then fold through to combine.

BAKE

Pour the mixture into the tin then gently smooth the top with a spatula. Promptly place in the oven and do not open the oven until the baking time is almost up.

TEST FOR DONENESS

Judge when a sponge cake is cooked by sight and touch, never pierce it with a skewer. A sponge cake is cooked if fingerprints disappear when the cake is lightly touched in the centre and the cake is beginning to pull away from the sides of the tin.

COOL

Remove the sponge from the tin immediately after taking it out of the oven so it doesn't overcook. Turn the cake onto a cooling rack lined with an untextured tea towel to avoid leaving imprints. Peel off baking paper if used then cover with a second tea towel to prevent the cake from drying out.

FILL

Fill cooled cakes two hours in advance then store in an airtight container in the refrigerator. This allows the cream to set and the sponge cake to soften. Take the cake out of the refrigerator half an hour before serving and decorate with fresh fruit if desired.

STORE

Sponges are best eaten on the day they are made however leftovers will keep for a couple of days stored in an airtight container in the refrigerator.

PASSIONFRUIT SPONGE
SERVES 8 GFA

4 eggs
¾ cup (165g) caster sugar
¾ cup (115g) self-raising flour
¼ cup (35g) cornflour
2 tablespoons (40ml) boiling water
Fresh berries and edible flowers for decorating

Chantilly Cream
300ml (300g) thickened cream
1 tablespoon icing sugar
1 teaspoon vanilla bean paste

Passionfruit Icing
1½ cups (240g) icing sugar
60g butter
2 tablespoons (40ml) passionfruit juice

Preheat oven to 170°C. Grease and flour 2 x 20cm round cake tins.
Place eggs and sugar into the bowl of an electric mixer fitted with a whisk attachment. Beat on high speed for 15 minutes or until mixture is pale and thick and has tripled in volume.
TM Butterfly/15 minutes/Speed 3/MC off.
Sift self-raising flour and cornflour together twice. Gently fold flour through beaten eggs until incorporated.
TM Butterfly/40 seconds/Speed 1.
Add the boiling water and fold to combine.
TM Butterfly/20 seconds/Speed 1.
Divide the mixture between the two tins. Bake for 15 to 20 minutes or until fingerprints disappear when lightly touched.
Turn cakes out onto a cooling rack lined with a tea towel. Cover with a second tea towel and allow to cool.

Chantilly Cream
Place cream, icing sugar and vanilla into the bowl of an electric mixer fitted with a whisk attachment. Beat on medium-high speed until soft peaks form.
TM Butterfly/1 to 1.5 minutes/Speed 3.

Passionfruit Icing
Place all ingredients into a small mixing bowl and beat until smooth.
TM 40 seconds/Speed 4. Scrape halfway.
To assemble, sandwich sponges with Chantilly cream. Top with passionfruit icing then decorate with berries and edible flowers. Serve with leftover cream.

DIETARY ALTERATION
GF Self-raising flour = 115g GF self-raising flour.
Bake for 15 to 17 minutes.

GINGER FLUFF SPONGE
SERVES 8 GFA

4 eggs
¾ cup (165g) caster sugar
⅔ cup (100g) cornflour
¼ cup (35g) self-raising flour
3 teaspoons ground ginger
1 teaspoon mixed spice
1 teaspoon cocoa
1 teaspoon baking powder
1 tablespoon (30g) golden syrup
2 teaspoons boiling water
Rhubarb and ginger jam (pg. 174)
Cinnamon sugar for dusting

Honey Cream Filling
450ml (450g) thickened cream
1½ tablespoons (45g) honey

Preheat oven to 170°C. Grease and flour 2 x 20cm round cake tins.
Place eggs and sugar into the bowl of an electric mixer fitted with a whisk attachment. Beat on high speed for 15 minutes or until mixture is pale and thick and has tripled in volume.
TM Butterfly/15 minutes/Speed 3/MC off.
Sift cornflour, self-raising flour, ginger, mixed spice, cocoa and baking powder together twice. Gently fold flour through beaten eggs until incorporated.
TM Butterfly/40 seconds/Speed 1.
Mix golden syrup and boiling water together then fold into the batter.
TM Butterfly/20 seconds/Speed 1.
Divide the mixture between the two tins. Bake for 16 to 18 minutes or until fingerprints disappear when lightly touched.
Turn cakes out onto a cooling rack lined with a tea towel. Cover with a second tea towel and allow to cool.

Honey Cream Filling
Place cream and honey into the bowl of an electric mixer fitted with a whisk attachment. Beat on medium-high speed until soft peaks form.
TM Butterfly/1 to 1.5 minutes/Speed 3.
To assemble, sandwich sponges with rhubarb and ginger jam and honey cream. Top with remaining cream and dust with cinnamon sugar to serve.

DIETARY ALTERATIONS
GF Self-raising flour = 35g GF self-raising flour.

JAM ROLL
SERVES 8 GFA

4 eggs
½ cup (110g) caster sugar
½ cup (75g) cornflour
¼ cup (35g) plain flour
1 teaspoon baking powder
1 tablespoon (20ml) boiling water
1 teaspoon vanilla essence
½ cup (160g) raspberry jam (pg. 174)
Icing sugar to dust

Chantilly Cream
300ml (300g) thickened cream
1 tablespoon icing sugar
½ teaspoon vanilla extract

Preheat oven to 170°C. Grease a 26cm x 32cm Swiss roll pan and line with non-stick baking paper.
Place eggs and sugar into the bowl of an electric mixer fitted with a whisk attachment. Beat on high speed for 15 minutes or until mixture is pale and thick and has tripled in volume.
TM Butterfly/15 minutes/Speed 3/MC off.
Sift cornflour, plain flour and baking powder together twice. Add dry ingredients to beaten eggs then gently fold through.
TM Butterfly/40 seconds/Speed 1.
Mix boiling water with vanilla then fold through egg mixture.
TM Butterfly/20 seconds/Speed 1.
Pour mixture into pan and lightly smooth the surface. Bake for 13 to 16 minutes until fingerprints disappear when lightly touched.
Turn cake out onto a cooling rack lined with a tea towel and peel off baking paper. Roll the hot cake and the tea towel up together, beginning at the shorter end. Place seam side down on cooling rack and allow to cool completely.

Chantilly Cream
Place cream, icing sugar and vanilla into the bowl of an electric mixer fitted with a whisk attachment. Beat on medium-high speed until soft peaks form.
TM Butterfly/1 to 1.5 minutes/Speed 3.
To assemble, unroll cake and use a palette knife to spread evenly with jam then cream. Reroll and trim ends. Dust with icing sugar to serve.

DIETARY ALTERATION

GF Plain flour = 35g GF plain flour.

HONEY ROLL
SERVES 8 GFA

4 eggs
½ cup (110g) caster sugar
½ cup (75g) plain flour
¼ cup (35g) cornflour
1 teaspoon mixed spice
½ teaspoon bicarbonate of soda
2 tablespoons (60g) honey
1 teaspoon butter

Honey Cream Filling
300ml (300g) thickened cream
1 tablespoon (30g) honey

Preheat oven to 170°C. Grease a 26cm x 32cm Swiss roll pan and line with non-stick baking paper.
Place eggs and sugar into the bowl of an electric mixer fitted with a whisk attachment. Beat on high speed for 15 minutes or until mixture is pale and thick and has tripled in volume.
TM Butterfly/15 minutes/Speed 3/MC off.
Sift plain flour, cornflour, mixed spice and bicarbonate of soda together twice. Fold gently into beaten eggs.
TM Butterfly/40 seconds/Speed 1.
Heat honey and butter until bubbling then fold through batter.
TM Butterfly/20 seconds/Speed 1.
Pour the mixture into the baking pan and lightly smooth the surface. Bake for 13 to 16 minutes or until fingerprints disappear when lightly touched.
Turn cake out onto a cooling rack lined with a tea towel and peel off baking paper. Roll the hot cake and the tea towel up together, beginning at the shorter end. Place seam side down on cooling rack and allow to cool completely.

Honey Cream
Place cream and honey into the bowl of an electric mixer fitted with a whisk attachment. Beat on medium-high speed until soft peaks form.
TM Butterfly/1 to 1.5 minutes/Speed 3.
To assemble, unroll cake and use a palette knife to spread evenly with honey cream. Reroll and trim ends.

DIETARY ALTERATION

GF Plain flour = 75g GF plain flour.

CHOCOLATE ROLL
SERVES 8 GF

4 eggs
½ cup (110g) caster sugar
½ cup (75g) cornflour
2 tablespoons (20g) cocoa
½ teaspoon bicarbonate of soda
1 tablespoon (30g) golden syrup
2 teaspoons boiling water
Fresh raspberries to decorate

Raspberry Cream
400ml (400g) thickened cream
¼ cup raspberry jam (pg.174)
½ teaspoon vanilla extract

Preheat oven to 170°C. Grease a 26cm x 32cm Swiss roll pan then line with non-stick baking paper.
Place eggs and sugar into the bowl of an electric mixer fitted with a whisk attachment. Beat on high speed for 15 minutes or until mixture is pale and thick and has tripled in volume.
TM Butterfly/15 minutes/Speed 3/MC off.
Sift cornflour, cocoa and bicarbonate of soda together twice. Gently fold through beaten eggs.
TM Butterfly/40 seconds/Speed 1.
Mix golden syrup and boiling water together then fold into the batter.
TM Butterfly/20 seconds/Speed 1.
Pour the mixture into the tin and smooth the surface using a spatula. Bake for 13 to 16 minutes or until fingerprints disappear when lightly touched.
Turn cake out onto a cooling rack lined with a tea towel and peel off baking paper. Roll the hot cake and the tea towel up together, beginning at the shorter end. Place seam side down on cooling rack and allow to cool completely.

Raspberry Cream
Place cream, raspberry jam and vanilla into the bowl of an electric mixer fitted with a whisk attachment. Beat on medium-high speed until soft peaks form.
TM Butterfly/1 to 1.5 minutes/Speed 3.
To assemble, unroll cake and use a palette knife to spread evenly with raspberry cream. Reroll and trim ends. Decorate with extra raspberry cream and fresh raspberries.

POWDER PUFFS
SERVES 8 GFA

4 eggs
¾ cup (165g) caster sugar
½ cup (75g) plain flour
⅓ cup (50g) cornflour
2 teaspoons baking powder

Strawberry Cream
600ml (600g) thickened cream
1/3 cup strawberry jam
1 teaspoon vanilla extract

Preheat oven to 180°C. Grease and line 3 baking trays with baking paper.
Place eggs and sugar into the bowl of an electric mixer fitted with a whisk attachment. Beat on high speed for 15 minutes or until mixture is pale and thick and has tripled in volume.
TM Butterfly/15 minutes/Speed 3/MC off.
Sift flour, cornflour and baking powder together twice then gently fold through beaten eggs.
TM Butterfly/1 minute/Speed 1. Scrape halfway.
Drop dessertspoons of mixture onto the trays 5cm apart. Bake for 6 to 8 minutes or until cakes are golden and spring back when lightly touched.
Allow to cool for 5 minutes then use a palette knife to gently remove powder puffs from baking paper. Transfer to a wire rack.

Strawberry Cream
Place cream, strawberry jam and vanilla into the bowl of an electric mixer fitted with a whisk attachment. Beat on medium-high speed until soft peaks form.
TM Butterfly/1 to 1.5 minutes/Speed 3.
To assemble, pipe or spread strawberry cream onto the base of half of the puffs. Sandwich with remaining puffs. Store in an airtight container in the refrigerator for 4 hours or overnight to soften. Dust with icing sugar before serving.

DIETARY ALTERATION
GF Plain flour = 75g GF plain flour.

BAKERS NOTES
If the mixture stands on the tray for too long it will lose its aeration so spoon mixture onto tray just before placing into the oven.

LAMINGTONS

SERVES 8 GFA

4 eggs
½ cup (110g) caster sugar
½ cup (75g) cornflour
¼ cup (35g) plain flour
1 teaspoon baking powder
40g butter, melted
2 cups (160g) desiccated coconut, to coat

Chocolate Icing

1½ cups (240g) icing sugar
⅓ cup (40g) cocoa
60g butter
100ml boiling water

Preheat oven to 170°C. Grease a 20cm x 30cm lamington tin and line with baking paper.
Place eggs and sugar into the bowl of an electric mixer fitted with a whisk attachment. Beat on high speed for 15 minutes or until mixture is pale and thick and has tripled in volume.
TM Butterfly/15 minutes/Speed 3/MC off.
Sift cornflour, plain flour and baking powder together twice. Gently fold flours through beaten eggs.
TM Butterfly/40 seconds/Speed 1.
Add melted butter and fold through.
TM Butterfly/20 seconds/Speed 1.
Pour mixture into tin and bake for 16 to 18 minutes or until fingerprints disappear when lightly touched.
Turn cake out onto a cooling rack lined with a tea towel then remove baking paper. Cover with a second tea towel and allow to cool. Wrap cooled cake in plastic wrap and freeze for a minimum of 2 hours.

Chocolate Icing

Place all ingredients into a bowl and mix until smooth and glossy.
TM 40 seconds/Speed 4. Scrape halfway.
To assemble, trim edges from the cake and cut into 12 squares. Coat in icing then toss in coconut. Place on a wire rack lined with baking paper to set.

DIETARY ALTERATION

GF Plain flour = 35g GF plain flour.

VARIATION

Jelly Lamingtons
Prepare an 85g packet of raspberry jelly according to packet directions, adding in a ½ teaspoon of gelatine.
Pour into a large, shallow dish and refrigerate for 30 minutes or until jelly is the consistency of unbeaten egg whites. Turn cakes over in jelly until well coated then toss in coconut.

BAKERS NOTES

Freezing the cake makes it easier to cut the cake into neat squares and helps the icing to set quickly. Lamingtons can be filled with jam and Chantilly cream after the icing has set.

BISCUITS

HOW TO CREATE BEAUTIFUL BISCUITS

PREPARE THE DOUGH

There are three methods for preparing biscuit dough.

1. The creaming method where the butter and sugar are beaten together before adding the eggs then the flour.
2. The food processor method where all ingredients are pulsed together until a dough forms. You can use the creaming method if you don't have a food processor but allow time for the dough to chill in the refrigerator if it is too soft to work with.
3. The melt and mix method where the wet ingredients are melted together then mixed with the dry ingredients.

ROLL INTO BALLS

Use a measuring spoon to scoop portions of the dough then roll into balls. This way the balls are even in size and bake consistently. If you bake biscuits regularly, I recommend investing in a cookie scoop because it makes this job a lot quicker and cleaner. Flatten balls lightly using fingertips or a floured fork before baking.

CUT OUT SHAPES

Roll out dough between sheets of baking paper or plastic wrap to prevent the dough from sticking to the bench. Ideally doughs should be evenly rolled out until they are between 4 and 6mm in thickness. This way the biscuits can bake through without overcooking on the edges.

Chilling the dough in the refrigerator or freezer before cutting makes it easier to cut neat shapes and to transfer them to baking trays. Dough scraps can be rerolled, chilled and cut as necessary.

BAKE

Bake biscuits on flat trays with low or no sides and line them with baking paper so the biscuits don't stick. Biscuits will expand as they bake so space the dough 5cm apart to avoid ending up with one giant biscuit. If the biscuits are browning unevenly, rotate the tray 180° half way through the cooking time.

TEST FOR DONENESS

It can be difficult to tell when biscuits are cooked and just a couple of minutes makes all the difference between them being soft and chewy or hard and crunchy. To combat this problem, bake a small test batch and make a record of the ideal cooking time for your oven.

Generally, cooked biscuits feel firm around the edges when pushed. The top and bottom should be consistently coloured with the edges being slightly more golden.

COOL

Biscuits will be soft when they are removed from the oven and will firm up as they cool. Allow them to sit on trays for 5 minutes to set before transferring to a wire rack so they don't crumble.

STORE

To prolong their freshness, store biscuits in an airtight glass jar in a cool, dry place as soon as they have cooled.

Unbaked dough can be kept in the refrigerator for a few days or in the freezer for 3 months. To store dough, roll it into balls or cut it into shapes then place in a zip-lock bag or an airtight container layered between sheets of baking paper. Allow frozen dough to defrost before baking.

DECORATE

This is a popular albeit messy pastime in our house. Here are some of the ways we like to embellish our biscuits;

- Dip them in melted chocolate or drizzle it on top.
- Decorate them with royal icing (pg. 172).
- Cut out fondant shapes then stick them on with a light brushing of water.
- Sandwich two biscuits together with chocolate ganache, jam, basic icing or Dulce De Leche.

BASIC BISCUITS
MAKES 36 GFA VA

180g butter
⅔ cup (150g) brown sugar
⅓ cup (75g) sugar
1 egg
2 teaspoons vanilla extract
2 cups (300g) plain flour
½ teaspoon baking powder
Additional flavourings and ingredients (pg.50-51)

Preheat oven to 170°C. Line 3 biscuit trays with baking paper.
Beat butter and sugars on low speed until combined.
TM 2 minutes/Speed 3.
Increase speed to medium. Beat until pale and creamy.
TM 1 minute/Speed 4.
Beat in egg and vanilla until incorporated.
TM 20 seconds/Speed 4.
Sift in flour and baking powder. Mix to form a soft dough.
TM 1 minute/Closed Lid/Knead.
Knead any additional ingredients through the dough.
TM 20 - 40 seconds/Reverse/Speed 3.
Roll 3 teaspoons of mixture into balls. Place on baking trays and flatten slightly.
Bake for 12 to 14 minutes or until golden. Stand for 5 minutes then transfer to a wire rack to cool.

DIETARY ALTERATIONS

GF Plain flour = 300g GF plain flour.
V Butter = vegan butter.
Egg = 1 tablespoon (15g) custard powder + 2 tablespoons (40ml) water.

BAKERS NOTES

This is a great recipe to fill up the biscuit jar as it makes a big batch of biscuits which keep well. The dough can also be frozen then baked as needed.

Customise the biscuits by kneading up to 3 cups of additional ingredients through the dough. This can be a mixture of choc-chips, chopped chocolate, dried fruit, nuts, coconut, oats, muesli and seeds. 1 to 2 teaspoons of spice can also be added with the flour for additional flavour. For variety, divide the dough in half then add different ingredients to each portion.

Prepare any additional ingredients before making the dough. Also check to ensure any additional ingredients are suitable for people with dietary restrictions.

ADDITIONAL FLAVOURINGS & INGREDIENTS

Choc-Chip Biscuits
Add 1 cup (190g) of choc-chips.

M & M Biscuits
Knead 1 cup (220g) of M & M's Minis through the dough.

White Chocolate & Macadamia Biscuits
Knead ⅔ cup of shredded coconut, 1½ cups (150g) of chopped macadamias and 150g of chopped white chocolate through the dough.

Apricot, Coconut & Oat Biscuits
Add ⅔ cup each of shredded coconut (50g), rolled oats (60g), white choc-chips (125g) and diced dried apricots (100g).

Cranberry, Pistachio & Cinnamon Biscuits
Add 1 teaspoon of cinnamon with flour. Knead through 1 cup (130g) of cranberries and 1 cup (140g) of pistachios.

Ginger Biscuits
Add 2 teaspoons of ground ginger with flour. Knead through 1 cup (220g) of chopped naked ginger.

Peanut Biscuits
Add ½ cup (140g) of smooth peanut butter with butter. Knead 1 cup (140g) of lightly salted, roasted peanuts through dough.

Cinnamon Biscuits
Add 2 teaspoons of cinnamon with flour. Roll balls in cinnamon sugar before baking.

Caramello Biscuits
Press a square of Caramello chocolate into each ball of dough then roll to enclose.

100s & 1000s Biscuits
Ice with pink royal icing (pg. 171) and sprinkle with hundreds and thousands.

Dotty Biscuits
Roll dough into balls then decorate with Smarties or a Chocolate Freckle before baking.

Fairy Biscuits
Roll balls in sprinkles before baking.

Muesli Biscuits
Add 3 cups of untoasted muesli.

CHEWY CHOCOLATE & PEANUT BISCUITS

MAKES 28 GFA VA

180g unsalted butter
2/3 cup (150g) brown sugar
1/3 cup (75g) sugar
1 egg
2 teaspoons vanilla extract
1 2/3 cup (250g) plain flour
1/2 teaspoon salt
1/2 teaspoon bicarbonate of soda
1/2 teaspoon cream of tartar
150g dark chocolate, cut into chunks
1 cup (140g) roasted, unsalted peanuts

Preheat oven to 160°C. Line 3 biscuit trays with baking paper.
Beat butter, brown sugar and sugar on low speed until combined.
TM 2 minutes/Speed 3.
Increase speed to medium and beat until pale and creamy.
TM 1 minute/Speed 4.
Add egg and vanilla and continue to beat until incorporated.
TM 20 seconds/Speed 4.
Sift in flour, salt, bicarbonate of soda and cream of tartar. Mix to form a dough.
TM 30 seconds/Closed Lid/Knead.
Knead chocolate and peanuts through the dough.
TM 20 seconds/Reverse/Speed 3.
Allow dough to rest in a cool place for an hour if time permits. Scoop tablespoons of mixture into balls. Place 5 cm apart on baking trays.
Bake for 12 to 14 minutes or until golden. Allow to stand for 5 minutes then transfer to a wire rack to cool completely.

DIETARY ALTERATIONS

GF Plain flour = 200g GF plain flour + 50g besan flour + 50g of cornflour.

V Use vegan butter and chocolate.
Egg = 1 tablespoon (15g) custard powder + 2 tablespoons (40g) soy milk.

VARIATIONS

Chewy Chocolate Chunk Cookies
Omit peanuts. Increase chocolate to 200g.

Chewy White Chocolate & Macadamia Biscuits
Substitute dark chocolate with white chocolate and peanuts with 1½ cups (150g) of chopped macadamia nuts.

Snickerdoodles
Add 2 teaspoons of cinnamon with flour. Omit chocolate and peanuts. Roll balls in cinnamon sugar before baking.

Red Velvet Cookies
Add 1 teaspoon of white vinegar and ½ teaspoon red gel food dye with vanilla and 2 tablespoons (20g) of cocoa with flour.
Replace dark chocolate and peanuts with 1 cup (190g) white choc-chips.

BAKERS NOTES

These biscuits are always a crowd pleaser with a crunchy edge and soft and chewy centre. They are best eaten on the day they are baked but the dough can be scooped into balls and stored in the refrigerator, ready to be baked as needed.

TRIPLE CHOCOLATE BISCUITS
MAKES 32 GFA VA

180g unsalted butter
2/3 cup (150g) brown sugar
1/3 cup (75g) sugar
1 egg
1 teaspoon vanilla extract
1 1/2 cups (250g) plain flour
1/2 cup (50g) cocoa
1/2 teaspoon bicarbonate of soda
1/2 teaspoon salt
100g white choc-chips
100g milk choc-chips

Preheat oven to 160°C. Line 3 biscuit trays with baking paper.
Beat butter, brown sugar and sugar on low speed until combined.
TM 2 minutes/Speed 3.
Increase speed to medium and beat until pale and creamy.
TM 1 minute/Speed 4.
Add egg and vanilla and continue to beat until incorporated.
TM 20 seconds/Speed 4.
Sift in flour, cocoa, bicarbonate of soda and salt and stir to combine.
TM 45 seconds/Knead.
Add choc-chips and mix through the dough.
TM 20 seconds/Reverse/Speed 3.
Roll tablespoons of mixture into balls and place on baking trays. Bake for 12 to 14 minutes or until firm around the edges. Allow to cool for 5 minutes before transferring to a wire rack to cool completely.

DIETARY ALTERATIONS

GF Plain flour = 225g GF plain flour + 25g cornflour.
V Use vegan butter and choc-chips.
Egg = 1 tablespoon (15g) custard powder + 2 tablespoons (40ml) water.

VARIATIONS

Chocolate Mint Biscuits
Replace choc-chips with 200g of chopped mint chocolate. After baking, drizzle with melted white and milk chocolate.

Chocolate, Hazelnut & Orange Biscuits
Replace choc-chips with 150g of chopped orange dark chocolate. Add 1 cup (140g) of chopped hazelnuts.

Chocolate, Cranberry & Coconut Biscuits
Replace milk choc-chips with 1 cup (75g) of shredded coconut and 1 cup (130g) of dried cranberries.

Chocolate Ginger Cookies
Add 1 tablespoon of ground ginger with flour. Replace choc-chips with 220g of chopped glacé ginger.

Chocolate Freckle Cookies
Omit choc-chips. Roll balls of dough in 100s & 1000s before baking.

CRISPY CHOC-CHIP BISCUITS

MAKES 32 GFA

180g unsalted butter
2/3 cup (150g) sugar
1/3 cup (75g) brown sugar
1 egg
1 teaspoon vanilla extract
1 1/3 cups (200g) plain flour
1/2 teaspoon salt
1/2 teaspoon bicarbonate of soda
1 cup (190g) choc-chips

Preheat oven to 140°C. Line 3 biscuit trays with baking paper.
Beat butter, sugar and brown sugar on low speed until combined.
TM 2 minutes/Speed 3.
Increase speed to medium. Beat until pale and creamy.
TM 1 minute/Speed 4.
Beat in egg and vanilla until incorporated.
TM 20 seconds/Speed 4.
Sift in flour, salt and bicarbonate of soda. Mix to form a smooth dough.
TM 30 seconds/Closed Lid/Knead.
Add choc-chips and knead through dough.
TM 20 seconds/Reverse/Speed 3.
Scoop tablespoons of mixture onto trays 10cm apart. Flatten slightly. Bake for 16 to 20 minutes or until golden brown.
Allow to cool on the tray for 5 minutes before transferring to a wire rack to cool completely.

DIETARY ALTERATIONS

GF Plain flour = 100g GF plain flour + 100g buckwheat flour.
V Use vegan butter and choc-chips.
Egg = 1 tablespoon (15g) custard powder + 2 tablespoons (40ml) water.

CORNFLAKE BISCUITS

MAKES 28 GFA VA

125g butter
1/2 cup (110g) sugar
1 egg
1 teaspoon vanilla extract
1 1/3 cups (200g) self-raising flour
3/4 cup (120g) sultanas
3 cups cornflakes, lightly crushed

Preheat oven to 170°C. Line two biscuit trays with baking paper.
Place butter and sugar into the bowl of an electric mixer and beat until pale and creamy.
TM 1 minute/Speed 4.
Add egg and vanilla extract and continue to beat until incorporated.
TM 20 seconds/Speed 4.
Add flour and sultanas and stir until combined.
TM 10 seconds/Reverse/Speed 4.
Place cornflakes into a shallow bowl. Scoop tablespoons of mixture into balls. Toss in cornflakes until well coated.
Place balls 4cm apart on prepared oven trays and flatten slightly. Bake for 14 - 16 minutes or until golden brown. Cool on trays for 5 minutes before transferring to a wire rack to cool completely.

DIETARY ALTERATIONS

GF Self-raising flour = 200g GF self-raising flour.
Use gluten-free cornflakes.
V Use vegan butter.
Egg = 1 tablespoon (15g) custard powder + 2 tablespoons (40ml) water.

BUTTERSCOTCH BISCUITS
MAKES 28

125g butter
½ cup (110g) dark brown sugar
1 egg yolk
2 teaspoons (15g) golden syrup
1 teaspoon vanilla extract
1¼ cups (190g) plain flour
2 teaspoons baking powder

Preheat oven to 160°C. Line 3 biscuit trays with baking paper.
Place butter and brown sugar into the bowl of an electric mixer and beat until pale and creamy.
TM 1 minute/Speed 4.
Beat in egg yolk, golden syrup and vanilla.
TM 10 seconds/Speed 4.
Add the flour and baking powder and bring together to form a dough.
TM 30 seconds/Closed lid/Knead.
Roll 2 teaspoons of mixture into balls and place on prepared trays. Flatten slightly using a fork.
Bake for 14 to 16 minutes, or until golden. Allow to stand on trays for 5 minutes before transferring to a wire rack to cool completely.

JAM DROPS
MAKES 32 GFA VA

125g butter
⅓ cup (75g) caster sugar
1 egg
1 teaspoon vanilla extract
1⅓ cups (200g) plain flour
½ teaspoon baking powder
Raspberry jam (pg.174)

Preheat oven to 150°C. Line 2 biscuit trays with baking paper.
Place butter and sugar into the bowl of an electric mixer and beat until pale and creamy.
TM 1 minute/Speed 4.
Add egg and vanilla and beat until incorporated.
TM 10 seconds/Speed 4.
Sift in flour and baking powder and mix to combine.
TM 10 seconds/Reverse/Speed 4.
Allow mixture to chill for 10 minutes in the refrigerator. Roll 2 teaspoons of mixture into balls and place on prepared trays, allowing room for spreading. Press a thumb into the middle of each ball of dough to make an indent. Fill each indent with jam.
Refrigerate for 30 minutes to help biscuits hold their shape. Bake for 20 to 25 minutes, or until golden and cooked through. Allow to cool on tray for 5 minutes before transferring to a wire rack to cool completely.

DIETARY ALTERATIONS

GF Plain flour = 150g GF plain flour + 1 cup (100g) almond meal.
V Use vegan butter.
Egg = 1 tablespoon (15g) custard powder + 2 tablespoons (40ml) water.

CUT-OUT COOKIES
MAKES 34 GFA VA

220g butter
¾ cup (165g) caster sugar
1 egg
1 teaspoon vanilla extract
2½ cups (375g) plain flour
½ teaspoon baking powder

Place butter and sugar into the bowl of an electric mixer and beat until creamy.
TM 1 minute/Speed 4.
Add egg and vanilla and beat until combined.
TM 20 seconds/Speed 4.
Add flour and baking powder and knead to form a dough.
TM 1 minute/Knead. Scrape halfway.
Roll out dough between two sheets of baking paper until 4mm in thickness. Refrigerate for a minimum of 1 hour.
Preheat oven to 150°C. Line 3 biscuit trays with baking paper.
Cut desired shapes from the dough and place on trays. Bake for 13 minutes until lightly golden and cooked through.
Allow to cool on trays for 5 minutes before transferring to a wire rack to cool completely.

DIETARY ALTERATIONS

GF Use 2 eggs.
Plain flour = 200g GF plain flour + 200g glutinous rice flour.
V Use vegan butter.
Egg = 1 tablespoon (15g) custard powder + 2 tablespoons (40ml) water.

VARIATIONS

Chocolate Cut-out Cookies
Reduce plain flour to 2 2/3 cups (350g) and add 1/2 cup (50g) cocoa powder.

GF Use 2 eggs.
Plain flour = 175g GF plain flour + 200g glutinous rice flour.

Vanilla and Chocolate Cookies
Prepare 1 x vanilla cookie dough and 1 x chocolate cookie dough. Cut out desired shapes from the doughs using a large cookie cutter. Using a smaller cutter, cut the middle from each shape and exchange the vanilla and chocolate centres.

Jam Hearts
Cut large hearts from the cookie dough. Using a smaller cookie cutter, remove the centre from half of the hearts. Bake and allow cookies to cool. Spread jam over large heart cookies and dust remaining cookies with icing sugar. Sandwich together.

Chocolate Oreo Cookies
Prepare chocolate cookie dough. Roll out until 3mm in thickness. Cut 4cm circles from the dough. Bake then allow to cool. Sandwich two biscuits together with basic vanilla icing (pg. 170).

BAKERS NOTES

These basic cookies can be shaped and decorated to suit any theme. Sandwich 2 biscuits together using dulce de leche, basic icing (pg. 170), chocolate ganache (pg. 173) or jam (pg. 174), decorate with royal icing (pg. 171) or dip in melted chocolate.

KINGSTON BISCUITS
MAKES 24 VA

180g butter
½ cup (110g) brown sugar
1 egg
2 tablespoons (60g) golden syrup
2 cups (300g) plain flour
¾ cup (60g) desiccated coconut
⅔ cup (60g) rolled oats
2 teaspoons baking powder

Chocolate Ganache
200g dark chocolate
200g sour cream

Preheat oven to 160°C.
Beat butter and sugar until pale and creamy.
TM 1 minute/Speed 4.
Add egg and golden syrup and beat to incorporate.
TM 15 seconds/Speed 4. Scrape halfway.
Stir through flour, coconut, oats and baking powder.
TM 15 seconds/Reverse/Speed 4.
Roll 2 teaspoons of mixture into balls. Place on lined baking trays and flatten slightly. Bake for 16 to 18 minutes until golden. Stand for 5 minutes then transfer to a wire rack to cool.

Chocolate Ganache
Melt chocolate.
TM 4 minutes/60°C/Speed 1.
Add sour cream. Beat until smooth.
TM 20 seconds/Speed 3. Scrape halfway.
Pipe icing onto the flat side of half of the biscuits and sandwich with remaining biscuits.

DIETARY ALTERATION

V Use vegan butter.
Egg = 1 tablespoon (15g) custard powder + 2 tablespoons (40ml) water
Chocolate ganache = 200g vegan chocolate + 200g coconut cream. Stand until mixture thickens.

VARIATION

Monte Carlo Biscuits
Omit rolled oats. Sandwich biscuits with basic vanilla icing (pg. 170) and raspberry jam.

GINGERBREAD BISCUITS

MAKES 28 GFA VA

125g butter
½ cup (110g) brown sugar
½ cup (175g) golden syrup
1 egg yolk
2½ cups (375g) plain flour
1 teaspoon bicarbonate of soda
1 tablespoon ground ginger
1 teaspoon mixed spice
Royal icing (pg. 171) to decorate

Beat butter and sugar with an electric mixer until well combined.
TM 40 seconds/Speed 4.
Beat in golden syrup and egg yolk until incorporated.
TM 20 seconds/Speed 4.
Sift in flour, bicarbonate of soda, ginger and mixed spice. Knead until mixture comes together.
TM 45 seconds/Knead.
Roll out dough between 2 sheets of baking paper until 5mm in thickness. Freeze for a minimum of 1 hour.
Preheat oven to 160°C and line 3 baking trays with baking paper.
Cut out desired shapes and place 3cm apart on baking trays. Bake for 8 to 10 minutes for soft biscuits or 14 to 16 minutes for crunchy biscuits.
Stand for 5 minutes then transfer to a wire rack to cool. Decorate with royal icing if desired.

DIETARY ALTERATIONS

GF Use 2 egg yolks.
Plain flour = 375g GF plain flour.
V Use vegan butter.
Egg yolk = 1 tablespoon (15g) custard powder + 2 tablespoons (40ml) water.

HONEY SNAPS

MAKES 24 -30 GFA VA

1 cup (150g) plain flour
1 cup (150g) wholemeal spelt flour
125g cold butter
⅓ cup (120g) honey
¼ cup (55g) caster sugar
1 teaspoon cinnamon
1 teaspoon mixed spice
1 teaspoon bicarbonate of soda

Place all ingredients into the bowl of a food processor and process until mixture just comes together.
TM 20 seconds/Speed 5.
Tip mixture onto a sheet of baking paper and press together to form a smooth dough.
Roll out between 2 sheets of baking paper until 4mm in thickness. Place dough in freezer for 1 hour.
Preheat oven to 150°C and line 2 baking trays with baking paper. Use a cookie cutter to cut out desired shapes then place on trays.
Bake for 15 to 18 minutes depending on size.
Allow biscuits to cool on tray for 5 minutes before transferring to a wire rack to cool completely.

DIETARY ALTERATIONS

GF Plain flour = 150g GF plain flour.
Spelt flour = 150g buckwheat flour.
V Use vegan butter.
Honey = 120g maple syrup.

ANZAC BISCUITS
MAKES 24 VA

1½ cups (135g) rolled oats
1 cup (150g) self-raising flour
¾ cup (165g) sugar
¾ cup (60g) desiccated coconut
180g butter
2 tablespoons (60g) golden syrup
1 tablespoon (20ml) boiling water
1 teaspoon bicarbonate of soda

Preheat oven to 170°C. Line 3 biscuit trays with baking paper.
Mix oats, flour, sugar and coconut in a large bowl.
TM 5 seconds/Reverse/Speed 3. Set aside.
Melt butter with golden syrup over a medium heat. Stir until butter has melted and mixture is warm.
TM 3 minutes/100°C/Speed 2.
Dissolve bicarbonate of soda in boiling water then stir into butter mixture.
TM 10 seconds/Speed 2.
Stir the butter mixture together with the oat mixture.
TM 15 seconds/Reverse/Speed 2.
Press tablespoons of mixture into balls. Place 5cm apart on trays. Bake for 8 to 10 minutes for chewy Anzacs or 14 minutes for crunchy Anzacs. Stand for 5 minutes then transfer to a wire rack to cool.

DIETARY ALTERATIONS

V Butter = 180g coconut oil.

VARIATION

Oat & Raisin Biscuits
Replace coconut with 2/3 cup (120g) raisins.

SNOWBALL COOKIES
MAKES 48

250g cold, unsalted butter
2 cups (300g) plain flour
1¼ cups (125g) ground almonds
½ cup (80g) icing sugar, plus extra for dusting
1 teaspoon vanilla extract

Preheat oven to 160°C. Line 2 baking trays with baking paper.
Place all ingredients into a food processor and process until mixture resembles fine breadcrumbs.
TM 15 seconds/Speed 5.
Continue to process in short bursts until mixture comes together and forms pea sized clumps.
TM 45 seconds/Closed lid/Knead.
Roll 2 teaspoons of mixture into balls. Place on baking trays and flatten slightly. Bake for 15 to 20 minutes or until lightly browned. Remove from oven and dust generously with icing sugar whilst still hot.
Allow to cool completely on trays.Tip cookies and icing sugar from the trays into a large zip lock bag and gently shake until cookies are well coated. Store in an airtight container.

YO-YO BISCUITS
MAKES 26 GFA VA

250g unsalted butter
1⅔ cup (250g) plain flour
½ cup (80g) icing sugar
½ cup (75g) custard powder

Passionfruit Icing
1½ cups (240g) icing sugar
60g butter
5 teaspoons passionfruit pulp

Preheat oven to 160°C. Line 3 biscuit trays with baking paper.
Place butter, flour, icing sugar and custard powder into the bowl of a food processor. Process until mixture resembles fine breadcrumbs.
TM 15 seconds/Speed 5.
Continue to process in short bursts until mixture just comes together and forms pea sized clumps.
TM 45 seconds/Closed lid/Knead.
Roll 2 teaspoons of mixture into balls. Place on trays and flatten slightly using a floured fork.
Bake for 13 minutes or until lightly golden. Stand for 5 minutes then transfer to a wire rack to cool.

Passionfruit Icing
Beat all ingredients together until smooth.
TM 40 seconds/Speed 4. Scrape halfway.
Pipe or spread the icing onto the flat side of half of the biscuits and sandwich with remaining biscuits.

DIETARY ALTERATIONS
GF Plain flour = 250g GF plain flour.
Custard powder = 90g GF custard powder.
V Use vegan butter and custard powder.
Bake for 16 minutes.

VARIATIONS

Lemon or Orange Yo-Yo Biscuits
Finely grate the rind of 2 lemons or 1 large orange into the food processor.
TM 20 seconds/Speed 9. Scrape halfway.
Add remaining dough ingredients and proceed with recipe. Use lemon or orange juice in place of passionfruit pulp in icing.

Melting Moments
Prepare icing using 1 tablespoon (20ml) of milk and 1 teaspoon vanilla extract in place of passionfruit pulp. Spread raspberry jam over the flat side of half of the biscuits and the vanilla icing over remaining biscuits. Sandwich jam biscuits with iced biscuits.

Chocolate Melting Moments
Reduce custard powder to 1/3 cup (50g) and add 1/3 cup (35g) cocoa.
For the icing use 1 tablespoon (20ml) of milk and 1 teaspoon vanilla extract in place of passionfruit pulp.

Coffee Melting Moments
Add 1 tablespoon of finely ground instant coffee with flour. For the icing, use 1 tablespoon (20ml) of milk and 1 tablespoon of cocoa in place of passionfruit pulp.

BASIC SHORTBREAD

MAKES 34 GFA VA

250g cold, unsalted butter
2¼ cups (340g) plain flour
½ cup (110g) caster sugar
1½ teaspoons vanilla extract

Place butter, flour, caster sugar and vanilla into a food processor and process until mixture resembles fine breadcrumbs.
TM 15 seconds/Speed 5.
Continue to process in short bursts until mixture comes together and forms pea sized clumps.
TM 45 seconds/Closed lid/Knead.
Add any additional ingredients and knead through the dough.
TM 20 seconds/Reverse/Speed 3.
Roll out the dough between two sheets of non-stick baking paper until 7mm in thickness. Refrigerate dough for 30 minutes.
Line three trays with baking paper. Use a cookie cutter to cut desired shapes, re-rolling the dough scraps as necessary. Place shapes on prepared trays and refrigerate for a minimum of 1 hour.
Preheat oven to 160°C. Bake for 15 to 20 minutes or until lightly golden around the edges and cooked through. Allow to cool on trays for 5 minutes before transferring to a wire rack to cool completely.

DIETARY ALTERATIONS

GF Plain flour = 300g GF plain flour + 100g cornflour.
V Butter = ¾ cup (160g) olive oil. Knead only. Bake for 20 minutes.

VARIATIONS

Lemon & Thyme Shortbread
Add 1 tablespoon of finely grated lemon zest and 1 tablespoon of fresh thyme leaves to dough.

Cranberry & Pistachio Shortbread
Knead ½ cup (65g) cranberries and ½ cup (70g) of pistachios through dough.
Drizzle with melted white chocolate to serve.

Chocolate-Chip Shortbread
Knead 2⁄3 cup (125g) of choc-chips through.

Traditional Shortbread
Reduce plain flour to 1 2/3 cups (250g) and add ½ cup (100g) rice flour. Omit vanilla.

BROWN SUGAR SHORTBREAD

MAKES 34 VA

250g cold, unsalted butter
2¼ cups (340g) plain flour
½ cup (110g) brown sugar

Place butter, flour and brown sugar into the bowl of a food processor. Process until mixture resembles fine breadcrumbs.
TM 15 seconds/Speed 5.
Pulse in short bursts until mixture just comes together in pea sized clumps.
TM 45 seconds/Closed lid/Knead.
Roll out dough between two sheets of baking paper until 5mm in thickness. Freeze for 1 hour.
Preheat oven to 150°C and line three trays with baking paper.
Cut out desired shapes, place on baking trays and prick with a fork.
Bake for 16 to 20 minutes until golden and cooked through. Stand on trays for 5 minutes then transfer to a wire rack to cool.

DIETARY ALTERATIONS

V Use 180g of vegan butter.
Mixture will be crumbly so knead the dough using hands until the mixture comes together to form a dough.

VARIATIONS

Cinnamon Shortbread
Add 3 teaspoons of ground cinnamon.

Orange & Chocolate Shortbread
Add 1 tablespoon of orange zest. Dip half of each shortbread into melted dark chocolate to serve.

Ginger Shortbread
Add 3 teaspoons ground ginger with flour. Knead 200g sliced, naked ginger through the dough.
TM 10 seconds/Reverse/Speed 3.

Cardamom & Rosewater Shortbread
Add 3 teaspoons each of ground cardamom and rosewater. Dip in melted white chocolate and sprinkle with chopped, toasted pistachios to serve.

Coffee Shortbread
Add 1 tablespoon of finely ground of instant coffee.

SLICES

HOW TO MAKE PERFECT SLICES

PREPARE THE TIN

Grease the tin with a cold cube of butter to hold the baking paper in place. Line the tin with a sheet of baking paper slightly larger the tin. This allows you to use the baking paper to lift the slice out of the tin.

MAKE AN EVEN BASE

To create neat layered slices, you need to create an even base. To do this, tip the mixture into the tin and roughly spread using a spatula. Cover the mixture with a sheet of baking paper. Use a flat bottomed glass or a fondant smoother to firmly push the mixture down then slide it backwards and forwards to ensure the base is even.

BAKE

Rotate slices 180° half way through the cooking time so they brown evenly. Like biscuits, slices will continue to firm once removed from the oven. Bake only until they feel set in the centre because they will become dry and crumbly if they are overcooked.

TOP WITH CHOCOLATE

Choose a good quality block of chocolate that you enjoy eating rather than cooking chocolate for slice toppings. Break the chocolate into small pieces so it melts quickly and evenly and add a touch of oil to stop the topping from cracking when it is cut.

Pour the melted chocolate over the base then tilt the tin to each corner until the chocolate has covered the entire slice. Tap the tray on the bench several times to remove any air bubbles then refrigerate to set.

ICE

Wait until slices have cooled before icing then use an offset palette knife to create a smooth topping.

REMOVE THE SLICE FROM THE TIN

Run a knife around the edges to release the slice from the tin then use the overhanging baking paper to lift out the slice.

CUT & SLICE

To cut slices into neat even pieces, firstly trim the edges. Cut the slice into 4 cm wide bars then cut each bar in half, then half again. Wipe the knife between cuts with a clean, damp cloth.

To cut slices with a chocolate topping, remove them from the refrigerator 10 minutes before cutting so the topping doesn't crack. Position a large, serrated knife on the surface of the slice. With one hand on the handle and the other at the top of the knife, slowly rock the knife up and down until you have cut through the chocolate then push down firmly with both hands to cleanly cut through the base.

STORE

Store slices in an airtight container between sheets of baking paper. Keep them in the refrigerator for up to 1 week or freezer for up to 3 months. Unfortunately Lemon Squares, Jelly Slice, Mars Bar Slice and Marshmallow Slice don't freeze well.

BASIC LAYERED SLICE BASE
MAKES ONE BASE GFA VA

125g butter
1 cup (150g) self-raising flour
¾ cup (60g) desiccated coconut
½ cup (110g) brown sugar

Preheat oven to 160°C. Grease and line a 27 x 17.5cm slice tin.
Melt butter.
TM 4 minutes/70°C/Speed 1.
Add the flour, coconut and sugar and mix thoroughly.
TM 20 seconds/Reverse/Speed 3. Scrape halfway.
Press mixture into tin and bake for 15 minutes until golden.
Remove from oven and press down edges to form an even base. Allow to cool.

DIETARY ALTERATIONS

GF Self-raising flour = 75g GF plain flour + 75g besan flour + 2 teaspoons baking powder.
V Use vegan butter.

VEGAN COCONUT CARAMEL SLICE
MAKES 24 PIECES V GF

1 x Basic layered slice base (see previous recipe)

Caramel Filling
¾ cup (155g) raw sugar
½ cup (120g) canned coconut milk
2 tablespoons (60g) golden syrup
50g vegan butter
1¼ cups (100g) desiccated coconut
1 teaspoon vanilla bean paste

Chocolate Topping
200g vegan dark chocolate, broken into squares
1 teaspoon vegetable oil

Caramel Filling
Place sugar, coconut milk, golden syrup, butter, desiccated coconut and vanilla into a saucepan over a medium heat. Cook, stirring continuously until liquid has evaporated and mixture is thick and sticky.
TM 15 minutes/Varoma/Speed 3/MC off.
Spread mixture over cooled slice base. Refrigerate until cold.

Chocolate Topping
Microwave chocolate and oil in 20 second bursts, stirring after each interval until chocolate is melted.
TM 4 minutes/60°C/Speed 1.
Pour topping over base. Refrigerate to set before cutting.

CARAMEL SLICE

MAKES 24 PIECES GF

1 x Basic layered slice base (recipe pg. 81)

Caramel Filling
1 x 400g tin condensed milk
2 tablespoons (60g) golden syrup
50g butter

Chocolate Topping
180g dark chocolate, broken into squares
1 teaspoon vegetable oil

Preheat oven to 160°C.

Caramel Filling
Place condensed milk, golden syrup and butter into a saucepan over medium heat. Bring to a simmer, stirring for 5 to 10 minutes until caramel has thickened and darkened in colour.
TM 4 minutes/70°C/Speed 3/MC off then 7 minutes/Varoma/Speed 3/MC off.
Pour over base and spread evenly using a spatula. Return to oven for 10 minutes until golden and bubbling around the edges. Refrigerate until cold.

Chocolate Topping
Microwave chocolate and oil in 20 second bursts, stirring after each interval until chocolate is melted.
TM 4 minutes/60°C/Speed 1.
Pour topping over base. Refrigerate to set before cutting.

MARSHMALLOW SLICE

MAKES 24 PIECES GF

1 x Basic layered slice base (recipe pg. 81)

Marshmallow Filling
100ml lukewarm water plus 80ml extra
3 teaspoons gelatine
1 cup (220g) caster sugar
1½ teaspoons vanilla extract
¼ cup raspberry jam

Chocolate Topping
180g chocolate, broken into squares
1 teaspoon vegetable oil

Marshmallow Filling
Place 100ml of water into a bowl. Stir in gelatine then set aside to bloom.
Stir sugar and extra 80mls of water in a saucepan over a medium high heat until mixture is clear. Boil rapidly for approximately 3 minutes without stirring until mixture reaches 116°C on a sugar thermometer.
TM 8 minutes/Varoma/Speed 1/MC off.
Add the gelatine mixture and bring to a rolling boil. The mixture will be very bubbly and foamy. Boil for 1 minute then remove from heat.
TM 2.5 minutes/Varoma/Speed 1/MC off.
Allow to cool completely. Beat on high speed for 7 to 10 minutes until mixture is thick and fluffy.
TM Butterfly/20 minutes/Speed 3/MC off.
Add vanilla extract and beat until well mixed.
TM Butterfly/20 seconds/Speed 3/MC off.
Spread jam then marshmallow filling over base then refrigerate until set.
Chocolate Topping
Microwave chocolate and oil in 20 second bursts, stirring after each interval until chocolate is melted.
TM 4 minutes/60°C/Speed 1.
Pour topping over base. Refrigerate to set before cutting.

JELLY SLICE
MAKES 35 PIECES GF

1 x Basic layered slice base (recipe pg. 81)

Filling
¾ cup (185g) boiling water
2 teaspoons gelatine
1 x 400g tin condensed milk
¼ cup (60g) lemon juice

Jelly Topping
1 packet (85g) strawberry jelly crystals
1 teaspoon gelatine
1 cup (250g) boiling water
1 cup (250g) cold water

Filling
Place boiling water into a bowl. Sprinkle over gelatine and stir until dissolved.
TM 1 minute/Speed 3.
Whisk in condensed milk and lemon juice.
TM 20 seconds/Speed 3.
Pour over base and spread to the corners. Refrigerate for 2 hours or until set.

Jelly Topping
Place jelly crystals and gelatine into a heatproof bowl. Add boiling water and stir until jelly crystals are dissolved.
TM 1 minute/Speed 2.
Stir in cold water.
TM 10 seconds/Speed 2.
Allow jelly to cool to room temperature before carefully pouring over the filling.
Refrigerate overnight before cutting into squares.

VEGAN JELLY SLICE
MAKES 35 PIECES V

1 x Basic layered slice base (recipe pg. 81)

Filling
¾ cup (185g) cold water
1 sachet Jel-it-in
1 x 320g tin sweetened condensed coconut milk
¼ cup (60g) lemon juice

Jelly Topping
400ml undiluted raspberry cordial
100ml cold water
2 sachets Jel-it-in

Filling
Place water into a saucepan. Sprinkle over Jel-it-in and stir until dissolved.
TM 20 seconds/Speed 3.
Whisk in condensed coconut milk and lemon juice.
TM 20 seconds/Speed 3.
Bring mixture to a boil stirring. Allow to boil for 1 minute then remove from heat.
TM 4 minutes/100°C/Speed 3.
Pour over base and refrigerate to set.

Jelly Topping
Place water into a saucepan. Sprinkle over Jel-it-in and stir until dissolved.
TM 20 seconds/Speed 3.
Stir in raspberry cordial.
TM 20 seconds/Speed 3.
Bring mixture to a boil stirring. Allow to boil for 1 minute then remove from heat.
TM 5 minutes/100°C/Speed 3.
Carefully pour jelly over filling. Refrigerate overnight before cutting into squares.

PASSIONFRUIT SLICE

MAKES 24 PIECES GF VA

1 x Basic layered slice base (recipe pg. 81)

Topping

8 to 12 passionfruit to yield ½ cup (125ml) passionfruit juice
1 x 400g tin condensed milk
1 tablespoon (20g) lemon juice

Preheat oven to 160°C.
Halve passionfruit and scoop the pulp into a bowl. Whisk vigorously to separate the juice from the seeds.
TM 30 seconds/Reverse/Speed 5.
Pour the pulp through a fine sieve.
Measure out 125ml of passionfruit juice and reserve 1 tablespoon of seeds.
Pour passionfruit juice, reserved seeds, condensed milk and lemon juice into a bowl and beat until slightly thickened.
TM 30 seconds/Speed 4. Scrape halfway.
Pour mixture over base and bake for 10 minutes until mixture is set. Cool in the refrigerator before cutting.

DIETARY ALTERATION

Vegan Passionfruit Slice
Place ¼ cup (30g) of vegan custard powder and ¼ cup (55g) of sugar into a saucepan.
Gradually stir in ½ cup (125ml) passionfruit juice, 1 tablespoon (20ml) lemon juice and 1 cup (250ml) of coconut milk.
TM 10 seconds/Speed 5.
Stir over a medium heat for approximately 10 minutes until mixture thickly coats the back of a spoon.
TM 10 minutes/100°C/Speed 3/MC off.
Pour mixture over base and refrigerate until set.

APPLE & SOUR CREAM SLICE

MAKES 24 PIECES GF VA

1 x Basic layered slice base (recipe pg. 81)

Apple Filling

800g can pie apples
1½ tablespoons (20g) cornflour
1 tablespoon (20g) caster sugar

Topping

300ml (290g) sour cream
2 eggs
Cinnamon sugar for dusting

Preheat oven to 160°C.

Apple Filling
Stir cornflour and caster sugar through apples. Transfer to a colander and allow to drain whilst base is cooling.

Topping
Beat sour cream and eggs until combined.
TM 10 seconds/Speed 4.
Spread the apples evenly over the cooled base.
Pour sour cream mixture over apples and sprinkle with cinnamon sugar.
Bake for 25 to 35 minutes until just set.
Allow to cool then refrigerate until cold before cutting into squares to serve.

DIETARY ALTERATION

Vegan Apple Slice
Prepare apple filling. Spread over base and bake for 30 minutes at 160°C.
Place 2 tablespoons (40g) of sugar and 2 tablespoons (35g) of vegan custard powder into a saucepan. Gradually stir in 1 cup (260g) of soy milk. Bring to a simmer and cook, stirring, for 5 minutes or until mixture thickens.
TM 7 minutes/90°C/Speed 3.
Pour custard topping over baked apples. Allow to cool then refrigerate. Dust with cinnamon sugar to serve.

RASPBERRY & COCONUT SLICE

MAKES 24 PIECES GFA VA

Base

1½ cups (225g) self-raising flour
125g cold butter
⅓ cup (75g) sugar
1 egg
1 teaspoon vanilla extract
½ cup (160g) raspberry jam

Coconut Topping

1 egg
⅓ cup (75g) caster sugar
1 cup (80g) desiccated coconut
1 cup (75g) shredded coconut

Base

Preheat oven to 180°C. Grease and line a 27 x 17.5cm tin.
Process flour, butter and sugar until mixture resembles breadcrumbs.
TM 5 seconds/Speed 7.
Add egg and vanilla. Pulse until mixture forms clumps.
TM 10 seconds/Speed 5.
Press mixture into tin. Bake for 10 minutes until lightly golden. Allow to cool then spread with jam.

Coconut Topping

Whisk egg, sugar, desiccated coconut and shredded coconut together until well combined.
TM 30 seconds/Reverse/Speed 3.
Crumble coconut topping over jam. Bake for 10 to 20 minutes until golden. Refrigerate to cool before slicing.

DIETARY ALTERATIONS

GF Self-raising flour = 200g GF self-raising flour + 100g almond meal.
V Use vegan butter.
Base egg = 1 tablespoon (15g) custard powder + 2 tablespoons (40ml) of water.
Topping egg = 35ml aquafaba + 1 teaspoon vanilla extract

LEMON & COCONUT SLICE

MAKES 24 PIECES GFA VA

Rind of 2 lemons
250g packet Marie biscuits
1 cup (80g) desiccated coconut, plus extra to decorate
100g butter
½ tin (195g) condensed milk
2 tablespoons (40g) lemon juice

Lemon Icing

1½ cups (240g) icing sugar
60g unsalted butter
2 tablespoons (40g) lemon juice

Grease and line a 27 x 17.5cm slice tin.
Finely grate lemon rind into a mixing bowl.
TM 20 seconds/Speed 9. Scrape halfway.
Crush biscuits using a food processor.
TM 8 seconds/Speed 6.
Mix biscuits crumbs and coconut with lemon rind.
TM 10 seconds/Reverse/Speed 3. Set aside.
Melt butter with condensed milk and lemon juice.
TM 4 minutes/70°C/Speed 1.
Combine the butter mixture with the dry ingredients.
TM 20 seconds/Reverse/Speed 3.
Press mixture into tin. Refrigerate until firm.

Lemon Icing

Beat ingredients together until smooth.
TM 40 seconds/Speed 4. Scrape halfway.
Spread icing over base and sprinkle with extra coconut. Allow to set before slicing.

DIETARY ALTERATIONS

GF Marie biscuits = 280g GF Scotch Finger Biscuits.
Reduce butter to 60g.
V Marie biscuits = 250g Arnott's Nice biscuits.
Butter = 60g coconut oil.
Condensed milk = 160g sweetened condensed coconut milk.
Use vegan butter for icing.

LEMON SQUARES
MAKES 24 PIECES GFA

Base
125g butter
1 cup (150g) plain flour
¾ cup (60g) desiccated coconut
½ cup (110g) caster sugar

Lemon Topping
1½ cups (330g) caster sugar
4 eggs
2 egg yolks
1 cup (250g) lemon juice
⅓ cup (50g) plain flour

Base
Preheat oven to 160°C. Grease and line a 27 x 17.5cm slice tin.
Melt butter.
TM 4 minutes/70°C/Speed 1.
Mix in the flour, coconut and sugar.
TM 20 seconds/Reverse/Speed 3.
Press mixture firmly into the base and up the sides of the tin. Bake for 15 to 20 minutes until lightly golden.

Lemon Topping
Whisk the sugar, eggs, egg yolks and lemon juice together.
TM 20 seconds/Speed 4.
Sift in flour and whisk until smooth.
TM 10 seconds/Speed 4.
Carefully pour topping over warm base. Bake for 20 to 25 minutes until set in centre.
Allow to cool then refrigerate until firm. Dust with icing sugar to serve.

DIETARY ALTERATION
GF Base
Plain flour = 150g GF plain flour + 50g cornflour.
Topping
Plain flour = 50g cornflour.

VEGAN LEMON SQUARES
MAKES 24 PIECES V

Base
125g vegan butter
1 cup (150g) plain flour
¾ cup (60g) desiccated coconut
½ cup (110g) caster sugar

Lemon Topping
1½ cups (330g) caster sugar
¼ cup (35g) vegan custard powder
¼ cup (35g) tapioca flour
1 cup (240g) coconut milk
1 cup (250g) lemon juice

Base
Preheat oven to 160°C. Grease and line a 27 x 17.5cm slice tin.
Melt butter.
TM 4 minutes/70°C/Speed 1.
Mix in the flour, coconut and sugar.
TM 20 seconds/Reverse/Speed 3.
Press mixture firmly into the base and slightly up the sides of the tray. Bake for 15 to 20 minutes until lightly golden. Set aside to cool.

Lemon Topping
Place sugar, custard powder and tapioca flour into a saucepan. Gradually whisk in coconut milk and lemon juice.
TM 10 seconds/Speed 5.
Stir over a medium heat until custard thickly coats the back of a spoon.
TM 20 minutes/100°C/Speed 3.
Pour over base. Bake for 15 to 20 minutes.
Refrigerate overnight to firm before cutting into squares to serve.

DATE & PECAN SLICE

MAKES 24 PIECES GFA VA

1 cup (150g) self-raising flour
1 cup (160g) dried dates
1 cup (120g) pecans
125g butter
½ cup (110g) brown sugar
1 tablespoon (30g) golden syrup
1 egg
1 teaspoon vanilla extract

Preheat oven to 170°C. Grease a 27 x 17.5cm slice tray and line with baking paper.
Place flour and dates into a food processor. Pulse until dates are chopped.
TM 4 seconds/Speed 6.
Add pecans and pulse briefly to chop.
TM 2 seconds/Speed 5. Set aside.
Stir butter, sugar and golden syrup in a saucepan over a medium heat until butter has melted.
TM 4 minutes/70°C/Speed 1.
Whisk the egg and vanilla into the butter mixture.
TM 10 seconds/Speed 4.
Add flour mixture and stir until well combined.
TM 10 seconds/Reverse/Speed 3.
Spread mixture in tray. Bake for 20 minutes until golden and set. Cool in refrigerator before slicing.

BAKERS NOTES

Substitute the dates and pecans for 1 cup of dried fruit and 1 cup of chopped nuts or seeds of your choice. We like to use apricots and coconut for a nut-free version.

DIETARY ALTERATIONS

GF Self-raising flour = 75g GF plain flour + 75g besan flour + 2 teaspoons of baking powder.
V Butter = ½ cup (115g) mild olive oil.
Egg = 60ml soy milk mixed with 2 teaspoons psyllium husk + 1 teaspoon apple cider vinegar.

OAT BARS

MAKES 12 BARS VA

2⅓ cups (210g) rolled oats
1 teaspoon baking powder
⅓ cup (75g) brown sugar
¼ cup (55g) caster sugar
⅓ cup (65g) choc-chips or sultanas (55g)
125g butter
1 egg
1 teaspoon vanilla extract

Preheat oven to 170°C. Grease a 27 x 17.5cm slice tin and line with baking paper.
Place 120g of oats and baking powder into the bowl of a food processor. Mill to form a flour.
TM 30 seconds/Speed 9.
Stir oat flour together with remaining 90g of oats, brown sugar, caster sugar and choc-chips.
TM 10 seconds/Reverse/Speed 2. Set aside.
Melt butter.
TM 4 minutes/50°C/Speed 1.
Whisk egg and vanilla into melted butter.
TM 10 seconds/Speed 4.
Combine butter and oat mixtures.
TM 10 seconds/Reverse/Speed 3.
Spread mixture evenly into tin. Bake for 20 minutes until top is golden and slice feels set when touched.
Allow to cool in refrigerator before slicing into bars.

DIETARY ALTERATIONS

V Use vegan butter.
Egg = 40ml soy milk + 1½ tablespoons (15g) tapioca flour.

MUESLI BARS

MAKES 12 BARS GFA VA

⅓ cup (50g) self-raising flour
2 cups (180g) rolled oats
½ cup (65g) dried cranberries
½ cup (40g) shredded coconut
⅓ cup (55g) pumpkin seeds
⅓ cup (50g) sunflower seeds
2 tablespoons (25g) sesame seeds
1 tablespoon (15g) chia seeds
1 teaspoon cinnamon
⅓ cup (70g) mild olive oil
¼ cup (90g) honey
¼ cup (55g) brown sugar
1 teaspoon vanilla extract

Preheat oven to 160°C. Grease a 27 x 17.5cm slice tray and line with baking paper.
Stir flour, oats, cranberries, coconut, pumpkin seeds, sunflower seeds, sesame seeds, chia seeds and cinnamon together in a large mixing bowl.
TM 20 seconds/Reverse/Speed 2. Set aside.
Stir oil, honey, brown sugar and vanilla together in a saucepan over a medium heat until combined.
TM 3 minutes/80°/Speed 1.
Combine the oil mixture with the dry ingredients.
TM 20 seconds/Reverse/Speed 3.
Press mixture firmly into pan. Bake for 20 minutes until golden. Refrigerate to chill before slicing.

DIETARY ALTERATIONS

GF Self-raising flour = 50g GF self-raising flour.
Rolled oats = 2½ cups puffed brown rice.
V Honey = rice malt syrup.

CHOCOLATE BROWNIES

MAKES 25 PIECES GFA VA

125g butter
1 tablespoon (20g) mild olive oil
100g dark chocolate
¾ cup (165g) brown sugar
2 eggs
2 teaspoons vanilla extract
⅓ cup (75g) caster sugar
½ cup (75g) plain flour
2 tablespoons (25g) self-raising flour
½ cup (50g) cocoa powder

Preheat oven to 160°C. Grease a 20cm square cake tin and line with baking paper.
Place butter, olive oil, chocolate and brown sugar into a saucepan and stir over a medium heat until butter and chocolate are melted.
TM 4 minutes/70°C/Speed 1.
Whisk in eggs and vanilla.
TM 20 seconds/Speed 4.
Add caster sugar, plain flour, self-raising flour and cocoa and mix well.
TM 10 seconds/Speed 4. Scrape halfway.
Tip mixture into prepared pan and spread evenly.
Bake for 25 minutes until just set. Allow to cool in pan.

DIETARY ALTERATIONS

GF Plain flour = 75g GF plain flour.
Self-raising flour = 50g GF self-raising flour.
V Use vegan butter and chocolate.
Eggs = ¼ cup (60ml) aquafaba for fudgy brownies or
⅓ cup (80ml) aquafaba + 2 tablespoons (25g) custard powder for cakey brownies.

CHOCOLATE COCONUT SLICE

MAKES 24 PIECES GFA VA

150g butter
¾ cup (165g) brown sugar
1 egg
1 teaspoon vanilla extract
½ cup (75g) plain flour
⅓ cup (50g) self-raising flour
¾ cup (60g) desiccated coconut
2 tablespoons (20g) cocoa

Chocolate Icing

1½ cups (240g) icing sugar
60g butter
2 tablespoons (20g) cocoa
1½ tablespoons (30g) milk

Preheat oven to 160°C. Grease a 27 x 17.5cm slice tray and line with baking paper.
Melt butter with sugar over a medium heat.
TM 4 minutes/70°C/Speed 1.
Whisk in egg and vanilla.
TM 10 seconds/Speed 4.
Mix in flours, coconut and cocoa until well combined.
TM 20 seconds/Reverse/Speed 3.
Spread mixture into pan. Bake for 20 minutes until set. Allow to cool.

Chocolate Icing

Beat ingredients together until smooth.
TM 40 seconds/Speed 4. Scrape halfway.
Spread icing over base. Sprinkle with extra coconut.

DIETARY ALTERATIONS

GF Plain flour = 75g GF plain flour + 25g cornflour.
Self-raising flour = 50g GF self-raising flour.
V Butter = 125ml (115g) mild olive oil.
Egg = 2 tablespoons (20g) tapioca flour + 2 tablespoons (40g) soy milk.
Use vegan butter and milk in icing.

HEDGEHOG SLICE

MAKES 24 PIECES GFA VA

1 packet (250g) Marie biscuits
1¼ cups (125g) walnuts, roughly chopped
¾ cup (120g) sultanas
½ cup (40g) desiccated coconut
2 tablespoons (20g) cocoa
150g butter
½ cup (110g) brown sugar
2 tablespoons (60g) golden syrup

Chocolate Topping

180g milk or dark chocolate, broken into squares
1 teaspoon vegetable oil

Grease and line a 27 x 17.5cm slice tray.
Roughly crush biscuits, leaving some bigger chunks.
TM 5 seconds/Speed 4.
Add walnuts, sultanas, coconut and cocoa and stir to combine.
TM 10 seconds/Reverse/Speed 3. Set aside.
Melt butter with brown sugar and golden syrup.
TM 4 minutes/80°C/Speed 1.
Combine butter mixture with the dry ingredients.
TM 10 seconds/Reverse/Speed 4.
Press into tray and refrigerate until firm.

Chocolate Topping

Microwave chocolate and oil in 20 second bursts, stirring after each interval until chocolate is melted.
TM 4 minutes/60°C/Speed 1.
Pour topping over base. Refrigerate to set before cutting.

DIETARY ALTERATIONS

GF Marie biscuits = 280g GF Scotch Finger Biscuits.
V Marie biscuits = 250g Arnott's Nice biscuits.
Use vegan butter.

VARIATION

Rocky Road Hedgehog Slice
Exchange walnuts and sultanas for 1 cup (140g) of peanuts and 1 cup (65g) of mini marshmallows.

MARS BAR SLICE
MAKES 25 PIECES

4 x 53g Mars Bars, chopped
50g butter
1 tablespoon (30g) golden syrup
3 cups Rice Bubbles

Chocolate Topping
180g milk chocolate, broken into squares
1 teaspoon vegetable oil

Grease a 20cm square tin and line with baking paper.
Place Mars Bars, butter and golden syrup into a saucepan and stir over a low heat until melted. Allow to cool for 5 minutes.
TM 4 minutes/70°C/Speed 1.
Add rice bubbles and mix until combined.
TM 20 seconds/Reverse/Speed 2.
Gently press the mixture into the tin then refrigerate until firm.

Chocolate Topping
Microwave chocolate and oil in 20 second bursts, stirring after each interval until chocolate is melted.
TM 4 minutes/60°C/Speed 1.
Pour topping over base. Refrigerate to set before cutting.

MALT SLICE
MAKES 24 PIECES

1 packet (250g) Malt 'O' Milk biscuits
250g packet Maltesers
½ tin (195g) condensed milk
60g butter
2 tablespoons (60g) golden syrup

Chocolate Topping
180g white chocolate, broken into squares
1 teaspoon vegetable oil

Grease a 27 x 17.5cm slice tray and line with baking paper.
Crumb biscuits in a food processor.
TM 8 seconds/Speed 6.
Reserve 24 Maltesers for decorating. Halve remaining Maltesers and add to the biscuit crumbs. Stir to combine.
TM 10 seconds/Reverse/Speed 3. Set aside.
Place butter, condensed milk and golden syrup into a saucepan over a low heat and stir until butter has melted.
TM 4 minutes/70°C/Speed 1.
Combine condensed milk mixture with the crushed biscuits and mix well.
TM 20 seconds/Reverse/Speed 3.
Press mixture into prepared slice tray and refrigerate until firm.

Chocolate Topping
Microwave chocolate and oil in 20 second bursts, stirring after each interval until chocolate is melted.
TM 4 minutes/60°C/Speed 1.
Pour chocolate topping over base and decorate with reserved Maltesers. Refrigerate to set before cutting.

DAIRY MILK SLICE
MAKES 24 PIECES GFA VA

1 packet (250g) Marie biscuits
¼ cup (25g) cocoa
125g butter
½ tin (195g) condensed milk

Topping
180g chocolate, broken into squares
1 teaspoon vegetable oil

Grease and line a 27 x 17.5cm slice tray.
Crush biscuits with cocoa using a food processor.
TM 8 seconds/Speed 6. Set aside.
Melt butter with condensed milk over low heat, stirring until smooth.
TM 4 minutes/70°C/Speed 1.
Stir condensed milk and biscuit mixtures together.
TM 20 seconds/Reverse/Speed 3.
Press mixture into tin and refrigerate until firm.

Chocolate Topping
Microwave chocolate and oil in 20 second bursts, stirring after each interval until chocolate is melted.
TM 4 minutes/60°C/Speed 1.
Pour topping over base. Refrigerate to set before cutting.

DIETARY ALTERATIONS

GF Marie biscuits = 280g GF Scotch Finger Biscuits.
Reduce butter to 60g.
V Marie biscuits = 250g Arnott's Nice biscuits.
Butter = 60g vegan butter.
Condensed milk = 160g sweetened condensed coconut milk.

VARIATIONS

Caramello Slice
Melt a 180g block of Caramello chocolate with condensed milk and butter. Use Caramilk chocolate for topping.

Fruit & Nut Slice
Stir 1 cup (140g) of toasted slivered almonds and 1 cup (160g) of sultanas through biscuit crumbs.

Clinkers Slice
Roughly crush 300g of Clinkers.
TM 2 seconds/Speed 5.
Stir through biscuits crumbs.

Crunchie Slice
Roughly crush 200g of honeycomb.
TM 2 seconds/Speed 5.
Stir through biscuit crumbs.

Peppermint Slice
Roughly crumble 4 x Peppermint Crisp chocolate bars and stir through biscuit crumbs. Add ½ teaspoon of peppermint extract to condensed milk.

Snickers Slice
Melt a 180g block of Caramello chocolate with condensed milk and butter. Stir 1 cup (140g) of roasted peanuts through biscuit crumbs.

BAKERS NOTES

This is an indulgent no bake chocolate slice that makes a great gift. Follow the suggested variations or take some inspiration from your favourite chocolate bars to devise your own marvellous creation.

MUFFINS, SCONES & LOAVES

HOW TO BAKE GREAT MUFFINS

PREPARE THE TIN

Muffins love to stick so line the tin with muffin cases then spray the top of the tin and the inside of the muffin cases with non-stick baking spray.

MIX

Don't over-mix the wet and dry mixtures together or you will end up with tough muffins. Gently fold the wet ingredients into the dry ingredients until just combined. I do this by hand because it's quick and easy and keeps the muffins light.

FILL THE CASES

Save some time and mess by using a large ice-cream scoop to divide the batter evenly between the baking cases. The batter should almost reach the top of the cases, creating distinctive domed tops when baked.

BAKE

Bake in a moderately hot oven to help them rise. Muffins are cooked when a skewer inserted into the middle comes out clean.

COOL

Take the muffins out of the tin straight away so they don't sweat. Transfer to a wire rack to cool a little before serving but don't cover them or they will lose their crusty top.

STORE

Muffins are best devoured whilst still warm from the oven. Any leftovers can be left to cool then stored in an airtight container at room temperature for a couple of days or frozen for up to a month.

REHEAT

Refresh your muffins by popping them into a 160°C oven for 5 to 10 minutes to reheat.

APPLE & PECAN MUFFINS

MAKES 12 GFA VA

1 cup (150g) plain flour
1 cup (150g) wholemeal spelt flour
½ cup (110g) brown sugar
1 teaspoon baking powder
1 teaspoon bicarbonate of soda
2 teaspoons mixed spice
2 large apples, peeled and diced
½ cup (60g) pecans, chopped
1 cup (240g) buttermilk
½ cup (115g) mild olive oil
2 eggs
1 teaspoon vanilla extract
1 tablespoon raw sugar

Preheat oven to 180°C. Line a 12-hole muffin tin with baking cases then spray with non-stick baking spray.
Whisk flours, brown sugar, baking powder, bicarbonate of soda and mixed spice together in a large bowl.
TM 10 seconds/Reverse/Speed 3.
Toss apples and pecans through flour mixture.
TM 10 second/Reverse/Speed 2. Set aside.
Whisk buttermilk, oil, eggs and vanilla together.
TM 10 seconds/Speed 5.
Make a well in flour mixture then pour in wet ingredients. Fold together until just combined. Divide batter between the muffin holes then sprinkle over raw sugar.
Bake for 18 to 22 minutes or until a skewer comes out clean. Transfer to a wire rack to cool slightly.

DIETARY ALTERATIONS

GF Plain flour = 150g GF plain flour.
Spelt flour = 150g buckwheat flour.
V Buttermilk & Eggs = 2 teaspoons psyllium husk + 375ml soy milk + 30ml apple cider vinegar.
Mix then stand for 10 minutes before using.

CARROT & SULTANA MUFFINS

MAKES 12 GFA VA

1 cup (150g) plain flour
1 cup (160g) wholemeal plain flour
½ cup (110g) brown sugar
1 teaspoon baking powder
1 teaspoon bicarbonate of soda
1 teaspoon mixed spice
250g carrots, peeled
1 cup (100g) walnuts, chopped
¾ cup (120g) sultanas
1 cup (240g) buttermilk
½ cup (115g) mild olive oil
2 eggs
1 teaspoon vanilla extract
Cream cheese icing (pg. 171) to decorate

Preheat oven to 180°C. Spray a 12-hole muffin tin with non-stick baking spray.
Whisk flours, sugar, baking powder, bicarbonate of soda and mixed spice together in a large bowl.
TM 10 seconds/Speed 3. Set aside.
Grate carrots.
TM 4 seconds/Speed 5.
Stir carrot, walnuts and sultanas through flour mixture.
Whisk buttermilk, oil, eggs and vanilla together.
TM 10 seconds/Speed 5.
Make a well in flour mixture then pour in wet ingredients. Gently fold together until just combined.
Divide the mixture evenly between the muffin holes. Bake for 18 minutes or until a skewer comes out clean. Transfer to a wire rack to cool. Decorate with cream cheese icing.

DIETARY ALTERATIONS

GF Plain flour = 150g GF plain flour.
Wholemeal flour = 150g buckwheat flour.
V Buttermilk & Eggs = 2 teaspoons psyllium husk + 375ml soy milk + 30ml apple cider vinegar. Mix then stand for 10 minutes before using.

RHUBARB & GINGER MUFFINS

MAKES 12 GFA VA

1 cup (150g) plain flour
1 cup (150g) wholemeal spelt flour
½ cup (110g) sugar
1 teaspoon baking powder
1 teaspoon bicarbonate of soda
1 teaspoon ground ginger
100g naked ginger
1½ cups of rhubarb, cut into 1cm slices
1 cup (240g) buttermilk
½ cup (115g) mild olive oil
2 eggs
1 teaspoon vanilla extract
Extra sugar to sprinkle

Preheat oven to 180°C. Line a 12-hole muffin tin with baking cases then spray with non-stick baking spray.
Whisk flours, sugar, baking powder, bicarbonate of soda and ground ginger together in large bowl.
TM 10 seconds/Speed 3.
Finely chop naked ginger and add to flour.
TM Chop ginger with flour 3 seconds/Speed 7.
Toss sliced rhubarb through flour mixture.
TM 10 seconds/Reverse/Speed 2. Set aside.
Whisk buttermilk, oil, eggs and vanilla together.
TM 10 seconds/Speed 5.
Make a well in flour mixture then pour in wet ingredients. Gently fold together until just combined. Divide batter between the muffin holes and sprinkle with extra sugar.
Bake for 18 minutes or until a skewer comes out clean.
Transfer to a wire rack to cool slightly before serving.

DIETARY ALTERATIONS

GF Plain flour = 150g GF plain flour.
Spelt flour = 150g buckwheat flour.
V Buttermilk & Eggs = 2 teaspoons psyllium husk + 375ml soy milk + 30ml apple cider vinegar. Mix then stand for 10 minutes before using.

RASPBERRY MUFFINS

MAKES 12 GFA VA

¾ cup (90g) pecans
1 cup (150g) plain flour
1 cup (150g) wholemeal spelt flour
½ cup (40g) shredded coconut
½ cup (110g) sugar
1 teaspoon baking powder
1 teaspoon bicarbonate of soda
1 cup (240g) buttermilk
½ cup (115g) mild olive oil
2 eggs
1 teaspoon vanilla bean paste
1 cup (130g) raspberries

Preheat oven to 180°C. Line a 12-hole muffin tin with baking cases then spray with non-stick baking spray.
Finely chop pecans then set aside.
TM 1 second/Speed 5. Set aside.
Whisk together flours, coconut, sugar, baking powder and bicarbonate of soda in a large bowl.
TM 10 seconds/Reverse/Speed 3. Set aside.
Whisk together buttermilk, oil, eggs and vanilla.
TM 10 seconds/Speed 5.
Make a well in flour mixture then pour in wet ingredients. Mix until just combined.
Half fill muffin cases with batter then top with a few raspberries. Repeat with remaining batter and raspberries. Sprinkle over pecans.
Bake for 18 minutes or until a skewer comes out clean. Transfer to a wire rack to cool slightly before serving.

DIETARY ALTERATIONS

GF Plain flour = 150g GF plain flour.
Spelt flour = 150g buckwheat flour.
V Buttermilk & Eggs = 2 teaspoons psyllium husk + 375ml soy milk + 30ml apple cider vinegar.
Mix then stand for 10 minutes before using.

ORANGE & CHOCOLATE MUFFINS

MAKES 12 GFA VA

Zest of 1 orange
2 cups (300g) plain flour
½ cup (110g) sugar
1 teaspoon baking powder
1 teaspoon bicarbonate of soda
¾ cup (150g) choc-chips
½ cup (120g) sour cream
½ cup (125g) orange juice
½ cup (115g) mild olive oil
2 eggs

Preheat oven to 180°C. Line a 12-hole muffin tin with baking cases then spray with non-stick baking spray.
Finely grate orange zest into a large bowl.
TM 20 seconds/Speed 9. Scrape halfway.
Add flour, sugar, baking powder, bicarbonate of soda and choc-chips and whisk well to combine.
TM 10 seconds/Reverse/Speed 3. Set aside.
Whisk sour cream, orange juice, oil and eggs together.
TM 10 seconds/Speed 5.
Make a well in flour mixture then pour in wet ingredients. Gently mix together until just combined.
Divide the mixture evenly between the cases. Bake for 18 minutes or until a skewer comes out clean.
Transfer to a wire rack to cool slightly before serving.

DIETARY ALTERATIONS

GF Plain flour = 300g GF plain flour.
V Use vegan choc-chips.
Sour cream & Eggs = 2 teaspoons psyllium husk + 250ml soy milk.
Mix then stand for 10 minutes before using.

VARIATION

Orange & Poppy Seed Muffins
Replace choc-chips with 2 tablespoons of poppy seeds.

BANANA & OAT MUFFINS
MAKES 12 VA

Topping
1 cup (100g) walnuts
2 teaspoons maple syrup

Muffins
3⅓ cups (300g) rolled oats
2 teaspoons cinnamon
1 teaspoon baking powder
1 teaspoon bicarbonate of soda
1 cup (100g) walnuts
¼ cup (55g) brown sugar (optional)
1 cup (250g) very ripe banana
1 cup (260g) yoghurt
½ cup (115g) mild olive oil
⅓ cup (120g) honey or maple syrup
2 eggs
1 teaspoon vanilla extract

Topping
Place walnuts into a food processor. Pulse briefly to coarsely chop.
TM 3 seconds/Speed 4. Set aside.
Transfer to a small bowl. Add maple syrup and stir to combine.

Muffins
Preheat oven to 180°C. Line a 12-hole muffin tin with baking cases then spray with non-stick baking spray.
Place oats, cinnamon, baking powder and bicarbonate of soda into a food processor. Mill to form a flour.
TM 20 seconds/Speed 9.
Add walnuts and brown sugar. Pulse briefly to coarsely chop walnuts. Transfer mixture to a large mixing bowl.
TM 3 seconds/Speed 4. Set aside.
Blend banana, yoghurt, olive oil, honey, eggs and vanilla in the food processor until smooth.
TM 10 seconds/Speed 5.
Gently mix together the wet and dry ingredients until just combined.
Divide the mixture evenly between the muffin holes. Sprinkle over topping. Bake for 18 to 20 minutes or until a skewer comes out clean.
Transfer to a wire rack to cool slightly before serving.

DIETARY ALTERATIONS
V Yoghurt & Eggs = 2 teaspoons psyllium husk + 375ml soy milk + 30ml apple cider vinegar.
Mix then stand for 10 minutes before using.
Use maple syrup in place of honey.

HOW TO BAKE LIGHT SCONES

RUB IN THE BUTTER

Use really cold butter and only work it into the flour until it resembles breadcrumbs. This way, the butter won't melt until it hits the oven, creating little pockets of steam which make the scones light and fluffy. If you don't have a food processor, grate the butter into the flour then stir to combine. Also use cold liquids as this makes the dough firmer and easier to handle.

MIX

The key to making light scones is to mix the dough gently and handle it as little as possible. If you overwork the dough you will develop the gluten making the scones tough. Use a flat bladed knife to pull the ingredients together rather than vigorously stirring.

SHAPE

Dust the bench with just enough flour to prevent the dough from sticking. Sprinkle a little flour over the top of the dough and pat it out using floured hands to no less than 3cm in thickness. Gently rub the top and sides to smooth the dough and remove excess flour.

CUT

Spray the cutter with non-stick cooking spray then dip into a small bowl of plain flour before cutting. Press the cutter evenly into the dough and resist the urge to twist because this can cause the scones to rise unevenly. A gentle shake should then be enough to release the round of dough from the cutter. Dip the cutter in flour between cuts then continue to cut rounds from the dough as closely as possible to minimise scraps. Any scraps can be pushed together then reshaped and cut.

BAKE

Bake scones in a shallow tin lined with baking paper. Place them close together and bake at a high temperature because this helps them to rise quickly, making them light and fluffy. Brush with a little milk, buttermilk or cream prior to baking to encourage the top to brown. Scones are cooked when the top is lightly golden and they make a hollow sound when tapped.

SERVE

Wrap scones in a clean tea towel immediately after removing from oven to keep them moist and warm and to soften the crust. Serve warm with butter or jam and cream.

STORE

Scones are best eaten on the day they are baked whilst still warm from the oven. However, they do freeze very well. Seal cooled scones in zip lock bags and freeze for up to 3 months. Wrap scones in foil and place in a 160°C oven for 10 to 15 minutes to reheat.

LA BRACCESCA
LA BRACCESCA
LA BRACCESCA

LEMONADE SCONES
MAKES 12

2 cups (300g) self-raising flour
1 teaspoon baking powder
⅔ cup (165ml) lemonade, chilled
½ cup (120g) thickened cream
Plain flour for dusting and milk for brushing
Strawberry Jam (pg. 174) and Chantilly cream (pg. 171) to serve

Preheat oven to 200°C.
Sift flour and baking powder into a mixing bowl. Make a well in the centre then pour in lemonade and cream. Pull the ingredients together using a flat bladed knife.
TM 20 seconds/Closed lid/Knead.
Tip the dough onto a floured surface. Lightly dust with flour and pat out until 3cm in thickness. Grease and flour a 4.5cm cutter then cut rounds from the dough. Place on a lined baking tray and brush with milk. Bake for 13 minutes or until lightly golden. Remove from oven and wrap in a clean tea towel. Serve warm with jam and Chantilly cream.

DIETARY ALTERATIONS

GF Self-raising flour = 300g GF self-raising flour + 2 tablespoons (25g) cornflour.
Add a cold egg with lemonade and cream.
Use extra cornflour for dusting.
V Thickened cream = 1/3 cup (80g) coconut yoghurt + 2 tablespoons (40g) soy milk.

VARIATIONS

Currant Scones
Toss ½ cup (80g) of currants through flour before adding lemonade.

Blueberry & White Chocolate Scones
Toss 1 cup of frozen blueberries and ½ cup (100g) of white choc-chips through flour before adding lemonade.

GINGER SCONES
MAKES 9

2 cups (300g) self-raising flour
1 teaspoon baking powder
1 teaspoon ground ginger
1 teaspoon mixed spice
75g glacé ginger
⅔ cup (165ml) non-alcoholic ginger beer, chilled
½ cup (120g) thickened cream
Plain flour for dusting and milk for brushing
Butter to serve

Preheat oven to 200°C.
Whisk flour, baking powder, ground ginger and mixed spice together in a mixing bowl. Chop glacé ginger and stir through flour mixture.
TM 3 seconds/Speed 5.
Make a well in flour mixture and pour in ginger beer and cream. Pull a flat bladed knife through the ingredients until they come together.
TM 20 seconds/Closed lid/Knead.
Tip the dough onto a floured surface. Lightly dust with flour and pat out until 3cm in thickness. Grease and flour a 5.5cm cutter and cut rounds from the dough. Place on a lined baking tray and brush with milk. Bake for 15 minutes or until lightly golden. Remove from oven and wrap in a clean tea towel. Serve warm with butter.

DIETARY ALTERATION

GF Self-raising flour = 300g GF self-raising flour + 2 tablespoons (25g) cornflour.
Add a cold egg with ginger beer and cream.
Use extra cornflour for dusting.

WHOLEMEAL DATE SCONES
MAKES 9

1 cup (150g) self-raising flour
1 cup (160g) wholemeal flour
3 teaspoons baking powder
2 tablespoons (40g) brown sugar
1 teaspoon mixed spice
50g cold, unsalted butter
¾ cup (105g) Medjool dates, pitted
1 cup (250g) milk, plus extra for brushing
Plain flour for dusting
Butter to serve

Preheat oven to 200°C. Place flours, baking powder, sugar, mixed spice and butter into a food processor. Process until mixture resembles breadcrumbs.
TM 5 seconds/Speed 7.
Add dates and pulse until coarsely chopped.
TM 3 seconds/Speed 6.
Transfer mixture to a large bowl. Make a well in the centre and pour in milk. Gently pull the ingredients together using a flat bladed knife.
TM 20 seconds/Closed lid/Knead.
Tip dough onto a floured surface. Lightly dust with flour and pat out until 3cm in thickness. Grease and flour a 5.5cm cutter and cut rounds from the dough.
Place on a lined baking tray and brush with milk. Bake for 13 minutes until lightly golden and cooked through. Remove from oven and wrap in a clean tea towel.
Serve warm with butter.

DIETARY ALTERATIONS

GF Self-raising flour = 150g GF self-raising flour.
Wholemeal flour = 160g buckwheat flour.
Milk = 150ml milk + 2 eggs.
Dust with extra buckwheat flour.
V Use vegan butter.
Milk = ½ cup (125g) natural coconut yoghurt mixed with ½ cup (125g) soy milk.

BUTTERMILK SCONES
MAKES 9

2 cups (300g) self-raising flour
2 tablespoons (40g) caster sugar
1 teaspoon baking powder
Pinch of salt
40g cold, unsalted butter
1 cup (240g) buttermilk, plus extra for brushing
Plain flour for dusting
Strawberry Jam (pg. 174) and Chantilly cream (pg. 171) to serve

Preheat oven to 200°C. Place flour, sugar, baking powder, salt and butter into a food processor and process until mixture resembles breadcrumbs.
TM 5 seconds/Speed 7.
Transfer mixture to a large bowl. Make a well in the centre then pour in buttermilk. Pull a flat bladed knife through the ingredients until they come together.
TM 20 seconds/Closed lid/Knead.
Tip the dough onto a floured surface. Lightly dust with flour and pat out until 3cm in thickness.
Grease and flour a 5.5cm cutter. Cut rounds from the dough and place on a lined baking tray.
Brush with extra buttermilk. Bake for 12 to 14 minutes until lightly golden. Remove from oven and wrap in a clean tea towel. Serve warm with jam and Chantilly cream.

DIETARY ALTERATIONS

GF Self-raising flour = 300g GF self-raising flour.
Add a cold egg with buttermilk.
V Use vegan butter.
Buttermilk = ½ cup (125g) natural coconut yoghurt mixed with ½ cup (125g) soy milk.

BANANA BREAD
MAKES 1 LOAF

1¼ cups (310g) ripe banana, approximately 3 large
½ cup (115g) mild olive oil
½ cup (110g) brown sugar
2 eggs
2 tablespoons (40g) milk
1 teaspoon vanilla extract
2 cups (300g) wholemeal spelt flour
1 teaspoon bicarbonate of soda
1 teaspoon baking powder
1 teaspoon cinnamon
1 teaspoon mixed spice

Preheat oven to 180°C. Lightly grease a 22 x 12 cm loaf tin and line with baking paper.
Blend bananas, olive oil, brown sugar, eggs, milk and vanilla in a food processor until smooth.
TM 20 seconds/Speed 5.
Sift in flour, bicarbonate of soda, baking powder, cinnamon and mixed spice. Pulse until just combined.
TM 15 seconds/Speed 4. Scrape halfway.
Pour mixture into pan. Bake for 40 to 50 minutes until a skewer comes out clean. Stand for 5 minutes before turning out to cool. Serve fresh or toasted with butter.

DIETARY ALTERATIONS

GF Spelt flour = 200g buckwheat flour + 1 cup (100g) almond meal.
V Eggs & Milk = ¾ cup (185g) soy milk + 3 teaspoons apple cider + 2 teaspoons psyllium husk. Mix then stand for 10 minutes before using.

DATE & WALNUT LOAF
MAKES 2 LOAVES

1 cup (150g) plain four
1 cup (150g) self-raising flour
1 teaspoon mixed spice
1 cup (100g) walnuts
1 cup (140g) Medjool dates, deseeded
60g butter
⅔ cup (145g) brown sugar
1 teaspoon bicarbonate of soda
1 cup (250g) boiling water
1 egg

Preheat oven to 160°C. Grease and flour two nut roll tins. Secure bases and place tins upright on a baking tray.
Place flours, mixed spice and walnuts into a food processor. Pulse briefly to coarsely chop walnuts. Transfer to a mixing bowl.
TM 2 seconds/Speed 4. Set aside.
Place dates into the food processor bowl with 1 teaspoon of flour mixture. Pulse briefly to coarsely chop dates.
TM 5 seconds/Speed 6.
Mix dates, butter, sugar, bicarbonate of soda and boiling water in a heatproof bowl.
TM 30 seconds/Reverse/Speed 1.
Cover and set aside for 30 minutes.
Mix in egg and flour mixture.
TM 15 seconds/Reverse/Speed 2.5.
Divide the mixture between the tins and secure lids. Bake for 35 to 40 minutes or until a skewer comes out clean.
Remove lids and allow to stand in tins for 10 minutes before turning out onto a wire rack. Serve with butter.

DIETARY ALTERATIONS

GF Plain and self-raising flour = 150g GF self-raising flour + 150g buckwheat flour.
V Use vegan butter.
Egg = 1 teaspoon psyllium husk + 1 tablespoon (20ml) water. Mix then stand for 5 minutes.

PIKELETS
MAKES 24 GFA VA

20g butter
1½ tablespoons caster sugar
1 cup (240g) buttermilk
1 egg, lightly beaten
1 cup (150g) self-raising flour
½ teaspoon baking powder

Melt butter.
TM 2 minutes/60°C/Speed 1.
Whisk in sugar, buttermilk and egg. Sift in flour and baking powder and whisk until batter is smooth.
TM 20 seconds/Speed 4. Scrape halfway.
Heat a non-stick fry pan over medium heat and rub with a cold cube of butter to grease. Drop dessertspoons of batter onto pan and cook until bubbles appear on the surface. Flip and cook until lightly golden. Repeat with remaining batter, regreasing the pan between each batch.
Serve warm or cold with sweet or savoury toppings.

DIETARY ALTERATIONS
GF Self-raising flour = 150g GF self-raising flour.
Use 2 eggs.
V Use vegan butter.
Buttermilk & Egg = 250ml soy milk + 2 teaspoons tapioca flour + 2 teaspoons white vinegar.
Mix and stand for 5 minutes before using.

CINNAMON DONUTS
MAKES 12 GFA VA

75g butter
2 tablespoons (35g) vegetable oil
1 egg
1 teaspoon vanilla extract
½ cup (120g) buttermilk
⅓ cup (75g) sugar
¼ teaspoon mixed spice
1⅓ cups (200g) self-raising flour

Cinnamon Coating
60g unsalted butter, melted
⅔ cup (150g) caster sugar
2 teaspoons cinnamon

Preheat oven to 180°C. Grease a 12 hole donut pan.
Melt butter.
TM 3 minutes/70°C/Speed 1.
Whisk in vegetable oil, egg, vanilla and buttermilk.
TM 10 seconds/Speed 4.
Add the sugar, flour and mixed spice then whisk until smooth.
TM 15 seconds/Speed 4. Scrape halfway.
Transfer mixture to a piping bag. Pipe the mixture into the donut holes. Bake for 8 minutes or until cooked through. Transfer to a wire rack.

Cinnamon Coating
Mix caster sugar and cinnamon together in a bowl.
One at a time, brush donuts with cooled melted butter and toss in cinnamon sugar to coat.

DIETARY ALTERATIONS
GF Self-raising flour = 150g GF plain flour + 50g besan flour + 3 teaspoons of baking powder.
V Use vegan butter.
Buttermilk & Egg = 160ml soy milk + 2 teaspoons white vinegar + 1 tablespoon (10g) custard powder. Mix then stand for 5 minutes.

HOW TO BAKE SOFT & FLUFFY BREAD

ACTIVATE THE YEAST

Yeast lies dormant until it is hydrated and fed. Begin with lukewarm water or milk. It should feel neither hot or cold to the touch. The temperature is important because yeast will die if the temperature is too hot and won't activate if the temperature is too cold. Mix in the yeast and a little sugar which acts as food for the yeast. The mixture should be foamy after 5 to 10 minutes indicating that the yeast is active.

KNEAD

This is the process of stretching the dough to develop the gluten which gives the bread structure. Kneading can be done by hand or with the help of the Thermomix or a free standing mixer fitted with a dough hook. This will take will take between 5 and 10 minutes depending on the method used. After this time the dough should look smooth and slightly shiny and feel firm and elastic. To test if the dough has been kneaded enough, poke it with your finger. If the dough springs back quickly it is ready.

BULK FERMENTATION

This is the initial rise where the yeast is left to ferment and creates gases causing the dough to rise. Place the dough in a large mixing bowl then cover it with plastic wrap to trap in moisture and heat. Sit the bowl in a warm spot ideally where the temperature is approximately 28°C. The dough needs to double in size during this stage.

KNOCK BACK

This involves punching or pushing out the air that has accumulated during the bulk fermentation. To do this, make a fist with your hand and push down in the centre of the risen dough to deflate. Turn it out onto a bench and knead a few times.

SHAPE

This is the stage where the dough is formed into the shape it will be baked in. The dough needs to be rolled tightly to form tension so it holds its shape. Place the shaped dough into the tin or tray it will be baked in, ready for proving.

PROVE

This is the final rise before the dough is baked. Like bulk fermentation, the dough needs to be covered in plastic wrap and left to prove in a warm spot. The final rise should take approximately half the time of the initial rise. The dough may not quite double in size during this time.

BAKE

Make sure the oven is preheated so the dough can go straight in once it has finished proving. The bread should be consistently coloured when it is cooked.

STORE

Homemade bread does not contain any preservatives so it is best eaten on the day it is baked. Any leftovers can be stored in the freezer and defrosted when needed.

FINGER BUNS
MAKES 12 BUNS

375ml milk
1 tablespoon instant dry yeast
3 tablespoons caster sugar
40g unsalted butter
1 egg
4 cups (600g) bakers flour
2 teaspoons mixed spice
1 teaspoon cinnamon
1½ teaspoons salt
1 cup (160g) sultanas

Glaze
⅓ cup (55g) pure icing sugar
1 tablespoon (20ml) boiling water

Icing
2 cups (320g) icing sugar
25g butter
50ml boiling water
Pink food colouring
Desiccated coconut to sprinkle

Heat milk in a saucepan over low heat or in the microwave just until lukewarm.
TM 1 minute/37°C/Speed 2.
Stir in the yeast and 1 tablespoon of the caster sugar.
TM 20 seconds/Speed 2.
Set aside for 10 minutes. The mixture should be foamy after this time indicating that the yeast is active.
Place the yeast mixture into the bowl of an electric mixer fitted with a dough hook. Add the remaining sugar, butter, egg, flour, mixed spice, cinnamon and salt. Mix on low speed until combined.
TM 5 seconds/Speed 5.
Set the mixer to medium speed for 8 minutes or until the dough forms a ball around the dough hook and is smooth and elastic.
TM 8 minutes/Closed Lid/Knead.
Tip dough onto a bench and knead through sultanas.
Form the dough into a ball and place in a large bowl. Cover with plastic wrap and set aside in a warm place to ferment for 1 hour or until doubled in size.
Line a 36 x 26cm baking tin with non-stick paper.
Knock back the dough and divide it into 12 portions. Press each portion out to a rectangle. Roll up firmly to form a cylinder and tuck under the ends.
Place buns in tin and cover with plastic wrap. Set aside in a warm place to prove for 30 minutes. Meanwhile, preheat oven to 180°C.
Uncover buns and bake for 20 to 25 minutes or until golden brown.

Glaze
Stir the sugar and water until the mixture is clear. Remove buns from oven and brush with glaze immediately. Transfer to a wire rack to cool.

Icing
Mix the icing sugar, butter, water and food colouring together in a small bowl until smooth.
TM 20 seconds/Speed 3. Scrape and repeat.
Pipe icing onto cooled buns and sprinkle with coconut.

DIETARY ALTERATION
V Milk = 400ml soy milk.
Butter & Egg = 60g of vegan butter.
Use vegan butter in icing.

VARIATION
Hot Cross Buns
Roll dough into 12 balls rather than cylinders.
Before baking mix ½ cup (75g) plain flour with 80ml of water. Transfer paste to a piping bag and pipe crosses across buns.
Omit icing.

CINNAMON SCROLLS
MAKES 12

Dough
375ml milk
1 tablespoon instant dry yeast
3 tablespoons caster sugar
40g unsalted butter
1 egg
4 cups (600g) bakers flour
2 teaspoons mixed spice
1 teaspoon cinnamon
1½ teaspoons salt

Cinnamon Filling
75g butter, very well softened
¼ cup (55g) brown sugar
3 teaspoons cinnamon

Glaze
⅓ cup (55g) pure icing sugar
1 tablespoon (20ml) boiling water

Glacé Icing
1½ cups (240g) pure icing sugar
30ml boiling water
2 teaspoons butter
Pink food colouring

Heat milk in a saucepan over low heat or in the microwave just until lukewarm.
TM 1 minute/37°C/Speed 2.
Stir in the yeast and 1 tablespoon of the caster sugar.
TM 20 seconds/Speed 2.
Set aside for 10 minutes. The mixture should be foamy after this time indicating that the yeast is active.
Place the yeast mixture into the bowl of an electric mixer fitted with a dough hook. Add the remaining sugar, butter, egg, flour, mixed spice, cinnamon and salt. Mix on low speed until combined.
TM 5 seconds/Speed 5.
Set the mixer to medium speed for 8 minutes or until the dough forms a ball around the dough hook and is smooth and elastic.
TM 8 minutes/Closed Lid/Knead.
Form the dough into a ball and place in a large bowl. Cover and set aside in a warm place to ferment for 1 hour or until doubled in size.
Line 2 baking trays with baking paper.
Knock back the dough then roll out on a floured surface to form a 48 x 30cm rectangle.
Mix the cinnamon filling ingredients and spread over dough leaving a 1cm strip along the top. Cut the dough into 12 vertical strips. Roll each strip up to form a scroll and place 6 scrolls on each tray. Cover with plastic wrap and prove for 30 minutes. Meanwhile, preheat oven to 180°C.
Uncover scrolls and bake for 20 to 25 minutes or until golden brown.
Mix together boiling water and icing sugar to make the glaze. Brush glaze over hot scrolls then transfer to a wire rack to cool.
To make the glacé icing, sift icing sugar into a bowl. Add water and butter and mix to a paste.
TM 40 seconds/Speed 4. Scrape halfway.
Add in extra water a teaspoon at a time until desired consistency is reached. Drizzle over cooled scrolls.

DIETARY ALTERATION
V Milk = 400ml soy milk.
Butter & Egg = 60g of vegan butter.
Use vegan butter in filling and icing.

SAVOURY BITES

GOJI & COCONUT CRACKERS

MAKES 100 GFA VA

1 cup (160g) wholemeal flour
1 cup (150g) plain flour
1 cup (105g) goji berries
1 cup (75g) shredded coconut
¼ cup (55g) caster sugar
¼ cup (45g) flaxseed meal
¼ cup (40g) pumpkin seeds
1 teaspoon bicarbonate of soda
1 teaspoon baking powder
½ teaspoon salt
1 cup (260g) plain yoghurt
¼ cup (90g) honey

Preheat oven to 180°C. Grease two 10 x 20cm loaf tins.
Whisk flours, goji berries, coconut, sugar, flaxseed meal, pumpkin seeds, bicarbonate of soda, baking powder and salt together in a mixing bowl.
TM 10 seconds/Reverse/Speed 3.
Mix yoghurt and honey and then add to dry ingredients. Stir until well combined.
TM 40 seconds/Reverse/Knead.
Divide mixture between the tins and smooth the surface. Bake for 20 to 25 minutes until golden and skewer comes out clean. Remove from tins and allow to cool. Wrap in foil and rest in refrigerator overnight.
Preheat oven to 120°C. Use a large serrated knife to slice the loaves into 2mm thick pieces. Arrange slices in a single layer on baking trays. Bake for 20 minutes. Turn crackers over and bake for a further 10 minutes until golden and cooked through. Transfer to a wire rack to cool completely. Store in an airtight container.

DIETARY ALTERATIONS

GF Wholemeal flour = 160g buckwheat flour.
Plain flour = 150g GF plain flour.
V Yoghurt = 250g plain coconut yogurt.
Honey = rice malt syrup.

CHEESE BISCUITS

MAKES 50 GFA VA

50g Parmesan cheese
50g tasty cheese
1 tablespoon (15g) self-raising flour
⅔ cup (100g) plain flour
85g unsalted butter
1 teaspoon dried chives
½ teaspoon smoked paprika
¼ teaspoon salt

Preheat oven to 180°C. Line 2 baking trays with baking paper.
Place Parmesan cheese, tasty cheese and self-raising flour into the bowl of a food processor and process until finely grated.
TM 8 seconds/Speed 8.
Add plain flour, butter, chives, smoked paprika and salt. Process until mixture comes together and forms clumps.
TM 20 - 40 seconds/Speed 5.
Roll teaspoons of dough into balls and place on baking trays. Press down to flatten into discs 5mm in thickness. Bake for 15 minutes until golden and cooked through.
Transfer to a wire rack to cool then store in an airtight container.

DIETARY ALTERATIONS

GF Self-raising flour = 2 tablespoons (25g) buckwheat flour.
Plain flour = 100g GF plain flour.
V Parmesan cheese = 2 tablespoons nutritional yeast flakes.
Use vegan tasty cheese and butter.

SPINACH SLICE
MAKES 12 SLICES GF

2 tablespoons psyllium husk powder
100g tasty cheese
200g baby spinach
1 onion, peeled and halved
5 rashes short cut bacon, chopped
2 teaspoons (10g) plus ¼ cup (55g) olive oil
Salt and pepper
6 eggs
¼ cup (40g) pine nuts

Preheat oven to 160°C. Grease a 20 x 30cm slice tin and line with baking paper.
Place psyllium husk into a large mixing bowl. Grate cheese and add to psyllium husk.
TM 4 seconds/Speed 8. Set aside.
Chop spinach then add to cheese.
TM 2 x 100g batches 5 seconds/Speed 5. Set aside.
Chop onion.
TM 3 seconds/Speed 5.
Sauté onion and bacon with 2 teaspoons of olive oil and a pinch of salt until softened. Add to spinach.
TM 6 minutes/Varoma/Reverse/Speed 1. Set aside.
Season eggs with salt and pepper. Whisk together with remaining ¼ cup of olive oil.
TM 10 seconds/Speed 5.
Stir eggs into spinach mixture. Pour into pan and sprinkle over pine nuts. Bake for 30 to 40 minutes until golden and set.

CORN PIKELETS
MAKES 36 GFA VA

50g tasty cheese
1 cup (150g) plain flour
½ cup (85g) instant polenta
1 tablespoon chives, chopped
2 teaspoons baking powder
¼ teaspoon salt
¼ teaspoon cayenne pepper
300ml (290g) buttermilk
2 eggs
¼ cup (55g) olive oil

Grate cheese into a mixing bowl.
TM 7 seconds/Speed 8.
Add flour, polenta, chives, baking powder, salt and cayenne pepper and stir to combine.
TM 10 seconds/Speed 4.
Make a well in the centre of the flour mixture. Pour buttermilk, eggs and oil into the well. Whisk until combined.
TM 10 seconds/Speed 4.
Heat a non-stick fry pan over medium heat and rub with a cold cube of butter to grease. Drop dessertspoons of batter onto pan and cook on both sides until lightly golden. Repeat with remaining batter, regreasing the pan between each batch. Serve warm or cold.

DIETARY ALTERATIONS

GF Plain flour = 150g GF plain flour.
V Tasty cheese = 2 tablespoons nutritional yeast flakes.
Buttermilk & eggs = 200g of plain coconut yogurt + 200g soy milk + 2 teaspoons psyllium husk.

PUMPKIN & FETA MUFFINS

MAKES 12 GFA VA

400g butternut pumpkin
Olive oil spray
2 cups (300g) plain flour
1 teaspoon baking powder
1 teaspoon bicarbonate of soda
125g cold butter
½ teaspoon salt
1 tablespoon thyme, chopped
2 teaspoons parsley, chopped
150g Danish feta cheese, crumbled
1½ cups (360g) buttermilk
2 eggs
2 tablespoons (35g) olive oil

Preheat oven to 180°C. Peel and cut pumpkin into 1cm cubes. Spread pumpkin over a baking tray lined with baking paper. Spray with olive oil and roast for 20 minutes until tender. Set aside to cool.
Spray a 12-hole muffin tin with baking spray.
Place flour, baking powder, bicarbonate of soda, butter and salt into a food processor. Process until mixture resembles breadcrumbs. **TM 10 seconds/Speed 5. Set aside.**
Transfer flour mixture to a large mixing bowl. Toss through roast pumpkin, feta, thyme and parsley.
Place buttermilk, eggs and olive oil into the food processor bowl and whiz until combined. **TM 10 seconds/Speed 5.**
Make a well in flour mixture then pour in wet ingredients. Gently fold together until just combined.
Divide the mixture between the muffin holes. Bake for 22 to 28 minutes or until a skewer comes out clean. Transfer to a wire rack to cool slightly before serving with butter.

DIETARY ALTERATIONS

GF Plain flour = 300g GF plain flour.
V Butter = vegan butter.
Feta = 2 tablespoons nutritional yeast flakes.
Buttermilk & Eggs = 1 cup (250g) plain coconut yogurt + 1 cup (250g) soy milk + 1 tablespoon psyllium husk. Mix and stand for 10 minutes before using.

VARIATION

Cheese and Bacon Muffins
Exchange pumpkin, feta and thyme for 180g of diced bacon, 180g of grated tasty cheese and 2 tablespoons of chopped chives.

CHEESE PUFFS

MAKES 24 GF

80g tasty cheese
80g Parmesan cheese
160ml (160g) milk
60ml (55g) olive oil
1 egg
1¼ cups (170g) tapioca flour
1 teaspoon salt
2 tablespoons dried chives

Preheat oven to 200°C. Spray a 24 hole mini muffin tin with non-stick baking spray.
Grate cheeses into a the bowl of a food processor.
TM 10 seconds/Speed 9.
Add milk, oil, egg, tapioca flour and salt. Blend until smooth.
TM 20 seconds/Speed 8.
Spoon 3 teaspoons of batter into each muffin hole.
Bake for 15 to 20 minutes until puffed and golden.
Serve immediately.

CHEESE SCONES

MAKES 18 GFA VA

2 cups (300g) self-raising flour
120g tasty cheese
60g cold, unsalted butter
1 tablespoon chives, chopped
½ teaspoon salt
½ teaspoon paprika
200ml (200g) milk
Plain flour for dusting
Extra milk for brushing
20g Parmesan cheese, finely grated

Preheat oven to 200°C. Line a 30 x 20cm baking tin with baking paper.
Place the flour, cheese, butter, chives, salt and paprika into a food processor and process until mixture resembles breadcrumbs.
TM 5 seconds/Speed 7.
Tip flour mixture into a large bowl and make a well in the centre. Pour the milk into the well. Use a flat bladed knife to gently stir until the dough comes together.
TM 20 seconds/Closed lid/Knead.
Tip the dough onto a floured surface and dust with flour. Pat out until 3cm in thickness. Grease a 4cm cutter then dip into flour. Cut rounds from the dough, re-dipping the cutter in flour between each cut. Gently press the scraps of dough together and repeat.
Place the scones close together in prepared pan. Brush tops with milk and sprinkle with Parmesan cheese. Bake for 18 minutes until lightly golden. Remove from oven and wrap in a clean tea towel. Serve warm with butter or cream cheese.

DIETARY ALTERATIONS

GF Self-raising flour = 300g GF self-raising flour.
V Use vegan cheese, butter and milk.

PESTO PINWHEEL SCONES

MAKES 12 GFA VA

2 cups (300g) self-raising flour
60g cold butter
½ cup (120g) thickened cream
½ cup (125g) milk
½ cup basil pesto dip
120g tasty cheese, grated
Plain flour for dusting
Milk for brushing

Preheat oven to 200°C. Line a baking pan with non-stick baking paper.
Place flour and butter into a food processor. Pulse a few times until mixture resembles breadcrumbs.
TM 5 seconds/Speed 7.
Transfer flour mixture to a large bowl. Make a well in the centre then pour in cream and milk. Use a flat bladed knife to gently mix until the dough comes together.
TM 20 seconds/Closed lid/Knead.
Tip the dough onto a floured sheet of baking paper. Dust with flour and roll out to form a 25 x 35cm rectangle.
Spread the pesto over the dough then sprinkle with cheese.
Beginning at the longer side, roll the dough up to form a cylinder. Trim the edges then cut the dough into 12 pieces.
Place the rounds 6cm apart on the baking tray then brush with milk.
Bake for 15 to 20 minutes until golden and cooked through.

DIETARY ALTERATIONS

GF Self-raising flour = 300g GF self-raising flour + 20g glutinous rice flour.
Add an egg with cream and milk.
V Use vegan butter, pesto and melting cheese.
Cream & Milk = ½ cup (125g) coconut yogurt mixed with ½ cup (125g) soy milk.

PUMPKIN & TURMERIC SCONES

MAKES 9 V

300g pumpkin
2 tablespoons (35g) mild olive oil
1 teaspoon turmeric powder
½ teaspoon ground coriander
½ teaspoon ground cumin
½ teaspoon salt
2 tablespoons (35g) brown sugar
¼ cup (60g) water
2 teaspoons psyllium husk powder
2 cups (300g) self-raising flour
1 teaspoon baking powder
Plain flour for dusting
Milk for brushing
2 tablespoons pumpkin seeds

Preheat oven to 200°C. Line a 20cm square baking tin with baking paper.
Peel then grate pumpkin.
TM 6 seconds/Speed 5.
Place pumpkin into a frying pan with olive oil, turmeric, coriander, cumin and salt. Gently sauté over a medium-low heat until pumpkin is tender and broken down.
TM 10 minutes/100°C/Speed 2.
Allow pumpkin to cool for 20 minutes then whisk in brown sugar, water and psyllium husk.
TM 10 seconds/Speed 4.
Sift in flour and baking powder. Use a flat bladed knife to gently stir until the dough comes together.
TM 20 seconds/Knead.
Turn dough onto a floured surface and dust with flour. Pat out until 3cm in thickness. Grease and flour a 5.5cm cutter and cut rounds from the dough. Place in tin in a 3 x 3 array. Brush with milk and sprinkle with pumpkin seeds.
Bake for 15 minutes until golden and cooked through. Serve warm with butter.

CARAMELISED ONION TART

SERVES 6

3 red onions, peeled, halved and thinly sliced
2 tablespoons (35g) olive oil
¼ teaspoon salt
2 tablespoons (35g) brown sugar
1 tablespoon (20g) balsamic vinegar
1 sheet puff pastry
1 egg, lightly beaten
2 slices prosciutto, torn
40g blue cheese, crumbled
Toasted walnuts and baby rocket leaves to serve

Place onions, olive oil and salt into a frying pan over a medium-low heat. Cook gently, stirring occasionally, until onions are soft and translucent.
TM 20 minutes/Varoma/Reverse/Speed 1/ MC off.
Add sugar and balsamic vinegar. Cook for a further 10 minutes until onions are sticky and caramelised.
TM 10 minutes/Varoma/Reverse/Speed 1/ MC off.
Set aside to cool. Meanwhile, preheat oven 200°C.
Cut pastry sheet in half vertically. Lay one half on an oven tray lined with baking paper. Brush with egg then lay second half on top. Score a 1cm border around the edge of the pastry and prick the inside with a fork.
Lay a second sheet of baking paper and a baking tray on top of the pastry to weigh it down. Bake for 15 minutes until partially cooked. Remove top tray and baking paper.
Brush pastry all over with beaten egg. Spread 2⁄3 cup of caramelised onions inside the border. Bake for 10 minutes.
Add torn prosciutto slices and bake for a further 10 minutes or until pastry is golden brown. Sprinkle over blue cheese, toasted walnuts and rocket leaves to serve.

DIETARY ALTERATIONS

GF Use gluten-free puff pastry.
V Use vegan puff pastry and brush with melted vegan butter.
Omit blue cheese and prosciutto.

TOMATO & GOATS CHEESE TART

SERVES 6

250g cocktail truss tomatoes
2 teaspoons sugar
2 teaspoons (10g) olive oil
1 teaspoon balsamic vinegar
1 clove garlic, crushed
½ teaspoon salt
1 sheet puff pastry
1 egg yolk, lightly beaten
2 tablespoons pine nuts
60g goats cheese
Fresh rocket leaves and cracked black pepper to serve

Preheat oven 200°C. Line an oven tray with baking paper.
Halve tomatoes horizontally and place into a bowl. Add sugar, olive oil, vinegar, garlic and salt and stir to combine.
Cut pastry sheet in half vertically. Lay one half on tray. Brush with egg then lay second half on top. Score a 1cm border around the edge of the pastry and prick the inside with a fork.
Lay a second sheet of baking paper and a baking tray on top of the pastry to weigh it down. Bake for 15 minutes until partially cooked. Remove top tray and baking paper.
Brush pastry with beaten egg. Drain tomatoes and arrange cut side up inside the pastry border.
Bake for 20 to 30 minutes until pastry is golden brown and tomatoes are tender. Set aside on a cooling rack.
Meanwhile, spread pine nuts over an oven tray and bake for 5 minutes until golden and toasted.
Sprinkle pine nuts, goats cheese and rocket over tart and season with freshly cracked pepper.

DIETARY ALTERATIONS

GF Use gluten-free puff pastry.
V Use vegan puff pastry and brush with melted vegan butter.
Omit goats cheese.

PALMIERS
MAKES 20 GFA VA

Cheese & Chive Filling
45g tasty cheese
75g cream cheese
1 tablespoon chives, chopped
¼ teaspoon onion salt
Ground black pepper

1 sheet butter puff pastry
1 egg yolk
2 teaspoons milk

Cheese & Chive Filling
Grate tasty cheese into a mixing bowl.
TM 4 seconds/Speed 8.
Add cream cheese, chives, onion salt and season with ground black pepper. Beat until combined.
TM 10 seconds/Speed 5.
Preheat oven to 200°C. Line a baking tray with baking paper.
Lay pastry sheet out on a sheet of plastic wrap. Spread filling over pastry sheet, leaving a 1 cm border along the top and bottom edges. Roll the pastry sheet up from the bottom and down from the top until the two rolls meet in the middle. Wrap in plastic and place in the freezer for 10 minutes to allow the pastry to chill.
Mix egg yolk with milk. Brush the egg wash all over pastry. Cut pastry into 1 cm slices and place on baking tray. Bake for 10 to 15 minutes until pastry is puffed and golden.

DIETARY ALTERATIONS
GF Use gluten-free puff pastry.
V Tasty cheese & cream cheese = 45g vegan tasty cheese + 75g vegan cream cheese + 2 teaspoons savoury yeast flakes.
Use vegan puff pastry and brush with olive oil.

MINI QUICHE
MAKES 24 GFA

2½ sheets shortcrust pastry
75g tasty cheese
100g ham, shredded
1 tablespoon finely chopped chives
½ cup (125g) thickened cream
6 eggs

Preheat oven 180°C. Grease a 12 hole muffin pan.
Cut 12 rounds from the pastry using a 9cm pastry cutter. Press pastry rounds into pan holes.
Grate cheese.
TM 5 seconds/Speed 8.
Divide ham, cheese and chives between pastry cases.
Place cream and eggs into a bowl and season with salt and pepper. Whisk to combine.
TM 10 seconds/Speed 5.
Fill pastry cases with egg mixture, reserving leftover mixture.
Bake for 15 minutes until filling is just set. Invert quiches onto a baking tray lined with baking paper. Brush with leftover egg mixture and bake for a further 10 minutes until pastry is cooked through and golden. Transfer to a wire rack to cool.

DIETARY ALTERATION
GF Use gluten-free puff pastry.

VARIATIONS

Substitute ham for alternative fillings such as corn kernels, smoked salmon, sautéed mushrooms, diced tomato, caramelised onions, shredded spinach or diced roasted pumpkin. You can also use blue cheese or feta cheese in place of tasty cheese.

VEGETABLE ROLLS

MAKES 48 V GFA

1 small onion, halved
1 large carrot
100g broccoli florets
120g pumpkin
1 tablespoon (20g) olive oil
1 teaspoon salt
1 x 400g can chickpeas, drained and rinsed
2 tablespoons lightly dried parsley
2 tablespoons nutritional yeast flakes
1 tablespoon psyllium husk
Freshly cracked black pepper
2½ sheets puff pastry
Vegan butter, melted for brushing
Sesame seeds to sprinkle

Grate onion, carrot, pumpkin and broccoli using a food processor.
TM 6 seconds/Speed 5.
Place vegetables, olive oil and salt into a saucepan over a medium heat. Sauté until vegetables are tender.
TM 10 minutes/Varoma/Reverse/Speed 1/ MC off.
Allow to cool for 10 minutes.
Return mixture to the food processor. Add chickpeas, parsley, nutritional yeast flakes and psyllium husk. Season with pepper. Pulse until ingredients are well mixed.
TM 4 seconds/Speed 5.
Transfer mixture to a piping bag fitted with a 3cm nozzle. Cut pastry sheets in half and pipe along the longer edge. Roll up firmly to enclose filling. Cut each roll into 4 pieces. Wrap in plastic wrap and freeze for later use if preferred.
To bake, preheat oven to 200°C. Place rolls on lined baking trays. Brush with melted butter and sprinkle with sesame seeds. Bake for 25 minutes if fresh or approximately 40 minutes if frozen, until pastry is golden.

DIETARY ALTERATION

GF Use gluten-free puff pastry.

SAUSAGE ROLLS

MAKES 48 GFA

3 slices white bread (70g), frozen
1 small onion, halved
1 medium carrot
1 small zucchini
1 tablespoon (20g) olive oil
1 teaspoon salt
500g pork and beef mince
2 tablespoons dried parsley
1 tablespoon dried Italian herbs
Freshly cracked black pepper
3 sheets butter puff pastry
1 egg, lightly beaten

Grate bread into a large bowl to form breadcrumbs.
TM 7 seconds/Speed 7. Set aside.
Grate onion, carrot and zucchini.
TM 6 seconds/Speed 5. Scrape halfway.
Sauté vegetables with olive oil and salt over a medium heat until vegetables are tender.
TM 10 minutes/Varoma/Reverse/Speed 1/ MC off.
Allow to cool for 10 minutes. Mix vegetables with breadcrumbs, mince, parsley, herbs and pepper until well combined.
TM 1 minute/Reverse/Speed 4. Scrape halfway.
Transfer mixture to a piping bag fitted with a 3cm nozzle. Cut each pastry sheet in half vertically and pipe along the longer edge. Roll up firmly to enclose filling. Cut each roll into 8 pieces. Sausage rolls can be wrapped in plastic wrap and frozen at this point for later use.
To bake, preheat oven to 200°C. Place sausage rolls on lined baking trays. Brush with lightly beaten egg. Bake for 20 to 25 minutes if fresh or approximately 40 minutes if frozen, until pastry is golden and filling is cooked through.

DIETARY ALTERATION

GF Breadcrumbs = 2 tablespoons psyllium husk. Use gluten-free puff pastry.

CHEESE & BACON ROLLS
MAKES 12 VA

100ml plus 300ml lukewarm water
1 x 7g sachet dry yeast
2 teaspoons sugar
1½ tablespoons (30g) unsalted butter
4⅓ cups (650g) bakers flour
1½ teaspoons salt
300g cheese, grated
6 rashes bacon, diced

Place 100ml of water, yeast and sugar into the bowl of an electric mixer. Stir to combine.
TM 20 seconds/Speed 2.
Leave mixture to stand for 10 minutes. The mixture should be foamy after this time indicating that the yeast is active.
Add remaining water, butter, flour then salt to the yeast mixture. Use an electric mixer fitted with dough hook to mix on low speed to combine. Increase speed to medium-high. Knead for 8 to 10 minutes until a smooth ball forms and the dough becomes smooth and elastic.
TM 8 minutes/Closed Lid/Knead.
Tip dough onto the bench and form into a ball. Place dough into a large bowl and cover with plastic wrap. Sit the bowl in a warm spot for 1 hour or until dough has doubled in size.
Preheat oven to 180°C. Line two 20 x 30cm baking tins with baking paper.
Knock back the dough to remove air pockets. Divide the dough into 12 equal portions and roll into balls. Place 6 balls in each baking tray and press down to flatten slightly. Cover with plastic wrap and allow to prove in a warm spot for 30 minutes.
Scatter cheese and bacon over rolls. Bake for 20 minutes until golden and cooked through.

DIETARY ALTERATION
V Use vegan butter and melting cheese. Omit bacon.

VEGEMITE SCROLLS
MAKES 12 VA

100ml plus 300ml lukewarm water
1 x 7g sachet dry yeast
2 teaspoons sugar
1½ tablespoons (30g) unsalted butter
4⅓ cups (650g) bakers flour
1½ teaspoons salt
⅓ cup (95g) Vegemite
2 tablespoons (40g) butter, softened
300g cheese, grated

Place 100ml of water, yeast and sugar into the bowl of an electric mixer. Stir to combine.
TM 20 seconds/Speed 2.
Leave mixture to stand for 10 minutes. The mixture should be foamy after this time indicating that the yeast is active.
Add remaining water, butter, flour then salt to the yeast mixture. Use an electric mixer fitted with a dough hook to mix on low speed to combine. Increase speed to medium-high. Knead for 8 to 10 minutes until a smooth ball forms and the dough becomes smooth and elastic.
TM 8 minutes/Closed Lid/Knead.
Form the dough into a ball and place into a large bowl. Cover with plastic wrap and sit the bowl in a warm spot to ferment for 1 hour or until doubled in size.
Preheat oven to 180°C and line 2 baking trays.
Knock back the dough then roll out on a sheet of lightly floured baking paper to form a 48 x 30cm rectangle.
Mix the butter and Vegemite and spread over the dough leaving a 2cm strip along the top. Sprinkle over the cheese. Cut the dough into 12 vertical strips. Roll each strip up to form a scroll. Place six scrolls on each tray. Cover with plastic wrap and allow to prove in a warm spot for 30 minutes. Remove plastic wrap and bake for 20 minutes until golden and cooked through.

DIETARY ALTERATION
V Use vegan butter and melting cheese.

ICINGS & FILLINGS

SWISS MERINGUE BUTTERCREAM

GF

3 egg whites (100g)
200g caster sugar
200g unsalted butter
1 teaspoon vanilla extract
Pinch of salt
Food dye (optional)

Thermomix Method

Thoroughly clean TM bowl and butterfly. To do this, insert butterfly into TM bowl. Add 1 litre of water and 60ml of white vinegar.
Heat 10 minutes/Varoma/Speed 3.
Pour out vinegar solution. Rinse and dry all TM components.
Insert butterfly. Place eggs and sugar to TM bowl.
Whisk 15 minutes/80°C/Speed 3/MC off.
Set meringue aside.
Wash and dry bowl and butterfly.
Place cold butter into TM bowl.
Beat 2 minutes/Speed 3.
Scrape down sides of the bowl and under the blades.
Insert butterfly. Return meringue to TM bowl.
Whip 2 minutes/Speed 3.
Scrape down sides of the bowl and butterfly.
Add vanilla, salt and food dye if using.
Beat 1 minute/Speed 3.

Conventional Method

Fill a saucepan with 5cm of water and bring to a simmer over medium heat. Place egg whites and sugar into a heatproof bowl and set over the saucepan.
Whisk continuously until the sugar has completely dissolved and mixture feels hot. It should reach 75°C on a digital thermometer.
Transfer the syrup to the bowl of a stand mixer fitted with a whisk attachment. Beat on high speed for 20 minutes until the mixture cools to room temperature and is very stiff and glossy.
Meanwhile cut butter into 3cm cubes and allow to soften. Butter should give when pushed but still be cool to touch.
When the meringue is stiff, exchange the whisk for a paddle attachment and set mixer to a medium high speed. Begin adding the butter a few cubes at a time, allowing it to be incorporated before adding more. If the mixture begins to split, keep beating until it comes back together.
Once the butter has been incorporated, beat in the vanilla, salt and food dye if using.

BAKERS NOTES

Store icing in an airtight container in the refrigerator for 1 week or freeze for up to 2 months. To use, allow to thaw then beat until mixture comes to room temperature and is smooth.

VEGAN MERINGUE BUTTERCREAM

GF V

90ml aquafaba
1/8 teaspoon cream of tartar
340g pure icing sugar
340g vegan butter
2 teaspoons vanilla extract

Place aquafaba, cream of tartar and icing sugar into the bowl of an electric mixer fitted with a whisk attachment. Beat on medium-high speed for 5 minutes or until the sugar has dissolved.
TM Butterfly/5 minutes/Speed 3/MC off.
Add half of the butter and continue to beat until thickened. Mixture may appear curdled at this stage.
TM Butterfly/1 minute/Speed 3.
Add remaining butter and beat until mixture is smooth and thick.
TM Butterfly/30 seconds/Speed 3.
Beat in vanilla until incorporated.
TM Butterfly/30 seconds/Speed 3.

BUTTERCREAM ICING

GF VA

250g cold, unsalted butter
3 cups (480g) icing sugar
2 tablespoons (40g) milk
1 teaspoon vanilla extract
Food dye (optional)

Place butter into the bowl of an electric mixer. Beat on a medium-low speed until butter is soft and pale.
TM 2 minutes/Speed 3.
Add half of the icing sugar and beat until mixture is creamy and fluffy.
TM 3.5 minutes/Speed 3.
Add remaining icing sugar, milk, vanilla and food dye and beat until smooth.
TM Butterfly/1 minute/Speed 3.
Check the consistency of the icing. If the icing is too thick, beat in an extra tablespoon of milk and if it is too thin add an extra 50g of icing sugar.

DIETARY ALTERATION

V Use vegan butter and milk.

VARIATION

Chocolate Buttercream
Reduce icing sugar to 2 2/3 cups (430g) and replace with 1/2 cup (50g) of cocoa.

GLACÉ ICING
GF VA

1½ cups (240g) pure icing sugar
1½ tablespoons (30ml) boiling water
1 teaspoon butter, softened

Sift icing sugar into a bowl. Add butter then mix in water to a form a thick paste.
TM 40 seconds/Speed 4. Scrape halfway.
Continue adding extra water a teaspoon at a time until desired consistency is reached.

DIETARY ALTERATION
V Use vegan butter.

VARIATIONS
Vanilla
Add 1 teaspoon of vanilla extract.

Chocolate
Sift 2 tablespoons of cocoa with icing sugar.

Coffee
Dissolve 1½ teaspoons of coffee in boiling water before adding to icing sugar.

Lemon, Orange or Passionfruit
Replace water with fruit juice.

BASIC ICING
GF VA

1½ cups (240g) icing sugar
60g butter
1½ tablespoons (30g) milk

Place all ingredients into a bowl and beat until smooth.
TM 40 seconds/Speed 4. Scrape halfway.
Check the consistency. If the icing is too thick, beat in extra milk a teaspoon at a time until desired consistency is reached.

DIETARY ALTERATION
V Use vegan butter and milk.

VARIATIONS
Vanilla
Add 1 teaspoon of vanilla extract.

Chocolate
Add 2 tablespoons (20g) cocoa.

Coffee
Replace milk with 1 tablespoon of coffee dissolved in 1 tablespoon of boiling water.

Lemon or Orange
Replace milk with 1½ tablespoons (30ml) of juice.

Passionfruit
Replace milk with 2 tablespoons (40ml) of passionfruit pulp.

ROYAL ICING
GF VA

2¼ cups (360g) pure icing sugar
¼ teaspoon cream of tartar
2 egg whites

Sift icing sugar and cream of tartar into the bowl of an electric mixer.
TM 10 seconds/Speed 5.
Add egg whites and whisk on high speed until icing is thick and opaque.
TM Butterfly/4 minutes/Speed 3.
Add water ½ a teaspoon at a time until desired consistency is reached.

DIETARY ALTERATION
V Egg whites = 60ml aquafaba.

CREAM CHEESE ICING
GF

250g unsalted butter
250g cream cheese
3 cups (480g) icing sugar

Beat butter using an electric mixer until pale and smooth.
TM 2 minutes/Speed 3. Scrape halfway.
Add cream cheese and half of the icing sugar. Beat until mixture is creamy and fluffy.
TM 2 minutes/Speed 3. Scrape halfway.
Add remaining icing sugar and beat until smooth.
TM Butterfly/1 minute/Speed 3.

CHANTILLY CREAM
GF VA

300ml thickened cream
1 tablespoon icing sugar
½ teaspoon vanilla extract

Place cream, icing sugar and vanilla into a bowl and whisk using an electric mixer until soft peaks form.
TM Butterfly/1 to 1.5 minutes/Speed 3.

DIETARY ALTERATION
V Thickened cream = well chilled 300ml can coconut cream.

VARIATIONS
Honey Cream
Replace icing sugar and vanilla with 1 tablespoon (30g) of honey.

Raspberry or Strawberry Cream
Replace icing sugar with 2 tablespoons of raspberry or strawberry jam.

VEGAN CREAM CHEESE ICING
GF V

180g vegan butter
3½ cups (560g) icing sugar
2 tablespoons (40ml) soy milk
2 teaspoons apple cider vinegar
1 teaspoon vanilla extract

Place all ingredients into a mixing bowl and beat until smooth.
TM 20 seconds/Speed 4.

CARAMEL CREAM CHEESE
GF VA

150g cream cheese
100g salted butter
2/3 cup (145g) brown sugar
1 tablespoon (30g) golden syrup
1 teaspoon vanilla bean paste

Place all ingredients into the bowl of an electric mixer fitted with a paddle attachment. Beat on medium speed until smooth and creamy.
TM 1 minute/Speed 4. Scrape halfway.

DIETARY ALTERATION
V Cream cheese = Extra 150g vegan butter + 2 teaspoons apple cider vinegar.

CARAMEL GLAZE
GF

125g butter
1/2 cup (120g) thickened cream
1/2 cup (110g) brown sugar
1 teaspoon vanilla bean paste
3/4 cup (120g) icing sugar

Place butter, cream, brown sugar, and vanilla into a saucepan over medium heat. Stir until butter has melted and sugar has dissolved. Bring to the boil, stirring. Boil for 5 minutes or until sauce coats the back of a spoon.
TM 8 minutes/Varoma/Speed 2/MC off.
Sift in icing sugar and whisk well to combine.
TM 20 seconds/Speed 4.
Cool slightly before pouring over cooled cakes. Leftovers can be stored in a glass jar in the refrigerator and served with ice cream.

VEGAN CARAMEL GLAZE
GF V

1 x 320g tin sweetened condensed coconut milk
2 tablespoons (60g) golden syrup
50g vegan butter

Place all ingredients into a saucepan over a medium heat. Bring to the boil then remove from heat.
TM 7 minutes/Varoma/Speed 2.
Cool slightly before pouring over cooled cakes.
Leftovers can be stored in a glass jar in the refrigerator.

HOW TO MELT CHOCOLATE

Stove top method
Break chocolate into pieces and place into a heatproof bowl. Set the bowl over a saucepan of simmering water, ensuring the water doesn't touch the bottom of the bowl. Stir until the majority of the chocolate is melted then remove from heat and continue stirring until completely smooth.

Microwave method
Break chocolate into pieces and place into a microwave safe bowl. Microwave for 30 seconds then stir. Continue to cook in 20 second intervals, stirring at the end of each interval, until the majority of the chocolate is melted. Stir continuously until the remainder of the chocolate has melted and mixture is smooth.

Thermomix method
Break chocolate into pieces and place in TM bowl.
Melt 5 minutes/50°C/Speed 2.

CHOCOLATE GANACHE
GF VA

250g dark chocolate
1 cup (240g) thickened cream

Finely grate chocolate and place into a heatproof mixing bowl.
TM 5 seconds/Speed 9. Set aside.
Bring the cream to a simmer.
TM 3 minutes/90°C/Speed 1.
Pour cream over chocolate and allow to stand for 5 minutes. Stir gently until chocolate is melted and mixture is smooth. Allow mixture to cool, stirring occasionally until it reaches desired consistency.

DIETARY ALTERATION
V Use coconut cream in place of thickened cream.

STRAWBERRY JAM
GF V

500g strawberries
375g - 500g sugar
2 tablespoons (40ml) lemon juice

Wash, hull and dry strawberries. Halve any large strawberries. Place into a ceramic bowl then stir through sugar and lemon juice. Cover and allow to stand at room temperature overnight to allow strawberries to release their juice.
Sterilise jars and place a plate into the freezer to test for setting point.
Strain the juices into a heavy based saucepan. Bring to the boil and allow to boil rapidly for 5 minutes.
TM 10 minutes/Varoma/Reverse/Speed 2/MC off.
Add the fruit and boil for 15 to 25 minutes until fruit is tender and the jam has reached setting point.
TM 20 - 25 minutes/Varoma/Reverse/ Speed 1.5.
Remove any scum from the jam and allow to cool for 5 minutes before ladling into jars and sealing tightly.

VARIATION

Raspberry Jam
Replace strawberries with raspberries.

BAKERS NOTES

Setting point is reached at 105°C. To test for setting point without a thermometer, spoon a little jam onto the chilled plate. Allow to stand for 30 seconds then slide your finger through the jam. If the jam doesn't flood to fill the gap, the jam is ready.

RHUBARB & GINGER JAM
GF V

500g rhubarb
375g sugar
2 tablespoons (40ml) lemon juice
1 tablespoon fresh ginger, finely grated
25g glacé ginger, finely sliced

Wash, dry and cut rhubarb into 2cm pieces. Place rhubarb into a ceramic bowl then stir through the sugar, lemon juice, fresh ginger and glacé ginger. Cover and stand at room temperature overnight to allow the sugar to dissolve and flavours to infuse.
Sterilise jars and place a plate into the freezer to test for setting point.
Transfer the mixture to a heavy based pan. Stir over a medium high heat until sugar has dissolved then bring the mixture to the boil. Boil, stirring regularly, until rhubarb is tender and setting temperature is reached.
TM 15 - 25 minutes/Varoma/Reverse/ Speed 1.5/MC off.
Remove any scum from the jam and allow to cool for 5 minutes before ladling into sterile jars and sealing.

LEMON CURD
GF

2 egg yolks
1 egg
1/3 cup (75g) sugar
1/3 cup (80g) lemon juice
100g cold, unsalted butter

Place egg yolks, whole egg and sugar into a heatproof bowl and whisk until combined.
TM Butterfly 2 minutes/ 37°C/Speed 4.
Add the lemon juice then set over a saucepan of simmering water. Cook, stirring over a medium-low heat until mixture begins to thicken.
TM Butterfly/2 minutes/80°C/Speed 4.
Add butter 1 cube at a time, stirring well after each addition. Continue to cook, stirring continuously until mixture is thick and coats the back of a spoon.
TM Butterfly/8 minutes/80°C/Speed 3.
For TM, replace measuring cup after adding each cube of butter to avoid splatters.
Pour into sterile glass jars and seal tightly. Allow to cool before storing in the refrigerator for 1 to 2 weeks.

VARIATION

Passionfruit Curd
Reduce lemon juice to 2 teaspoons and add 80ml of strained passionfruit pulp.

VEGAN LEMON CURD
GF V

1½ cups (330g) caster sugar
1/3 cup (40g) vegan custard powder
1 cup (240g) canned coconut milk
1 cup (250g) lemon juice

Place sugar and custard powder into a saucepan. Gradually whisk in coconut milk and lemon juice.
TM 10 seconds/Speed 5.
Stir over a medium heat until custard thickly coats the back of a spoon.
TM 15 minutes/100°C/Speed 3.
Pour into sterile glass jars and seal tightly. Allow to cool before storing in the refrigerator for 1 to 2 weeks.

LEMON SYRUP
GF V

1 cup (250g) strained lemon juice
3/4 cup (165g) sugar

Stir lemon juice and sugar over a medium heat until sugar dissolves. Increase heat and boil for 5 minutes or until mixture thickens and becomes syrupy.
TM 15 minutes/Varoma/Speed 3.

VARIATION

Orange Syrup
Replace lemon juice with orange juice.

BAKERS NOTES

WEIGHTS, MEASURES & CONVERSIONS

Standard Measurements

All recipes use standard Australian measurements.
All cup and spoon measurements are level.
Dry ingredients are loosely packed except for brown sugar which is firmly packed.

Liquid Measurements

Cup	Metric
1 teaspoon	*5ml*
1 tablespoon	*20ml*
¼ cup	*60ml*
⅓ cup	*80ml*
½ cup	*125ml*
⅔ cup	*160ml*
¾ cup	*180ml*
1 cup	*250ml*

Solid Measurements

Metric	Imperial
30g	*1 oz.*
55g	*2 oz.*
85g	*3 oz.*
115g	*4 oz.*
200g	*7 oz.*
225g	*8 oz.*
455g	*16 oz. /1 pound*

Ovens

The heat regulation in ovens varies greatly therefore use cooking times as a guide only. After trying some of the recipes, determine whether your oven is 'hot' or 'slow' in comparison. Adjust the temperature or baking time accordingly and take note of the time and temperatures that work in your oven.

Temperatures

All temperatures are in degrees Celsius.
Oven temperatures are for fan-forced setting.
Refer to the following guide for equivalent conventional oven settings.

Fan-Forced	Conventional
220°C	*250°C*
210°C	*240°C*
200°C	*230°C*
180°C	*200°C*
170°C	*190°C*
160°C	*180°C*
150°C	*170°C*
140°C	*150°C*
130°C	*140°C*
120°C	*130°C*
110°C	*120°C*
100°C	*110°C*
90°C	*100°C*

Equivalent Cake Pans

If you do not have the cake pan stated in the recipe, an alternative tin can be used if it holds the same volume as the original cake tin. The cooking time will need to be adjusted. If the new tin has a smaller surface area than the original tin, the baking time will be longer and if it has a larger surface area, the baking time will be shorter. Below are some appropriate substitutions.

20cm round tin;	*23cm round tin;*
20 cm x 10cm loaf tin	*20cm square tin*
12 hole muffin tin	*18 hole muffin tin*
	22cm x 12cm loaf tin

1 CUP WEIGHTS OF COMMON INGREDIENTS

Almonds, flaked	80 grams
Almonds, slivered	140 grams
Almonds, whole	160 grams
Almond meal	100 grams
Apricots, dried	150 grams
Aquafaba	250 grams
Banana, mashed	250 grams
Blueberries, fresh	150 grams
Buckwheat flour	150 grams
Buttermilk	240 grams
Cashews	150 grams
Cheese, Cheddar, grated	120 grams
Cheese, Parmesan, grated	80 grams
Choc-chips	190 grams
Cocoa powder	100 grams
Coconut, desiccated	80 grams
Coconut, flaked	50 grams
Coconut milk	240 grams
Coconut, shredded	75 grams
Corn flakes	40 grams
Cornflour	150 grams
Cranberries	130 grams
Cream, thickened	250 grams
Currants	160 grams
Custard powder	150 grams
Dates, dried, pitted	160 grams
Dates, fresh, pitted	150 grams
Figs, dried	150 grams
Flour, besan	150 grams
Flour, gluten-free	135 grams
Flour, plain	150 grams
Flour, rice	200 grams
Flour, spelt	150 grams
Flour, tapioca	140 grams
Flour, wholemeal	160 grams
Glucose	350 grams
Ginger, naked	200 grams
Golden syrup	360 grams
Hazelnuts	140 grams
Hazelnut meal	100 grams
Honey	360 grams
Jam	320 grams
Macadamias	100 grams
Maple syrup	235 grams
Milk	250 grams
Milk, soy	250 grams
Mini marshmallows	65 grams
Mixed peel	170 grams
Olive oil	230 grams
Peanuts	140 grams
Peanut butter	280 grams
Pecans	120 grams
Pine nuts	155 grams
Pistachios, ground	130 grams
Pistachios, shelled	140 grams
Polenta	170 grams
Prunes, deseeded	170 grams
Pumpkin seeds	170 grams
Raisins	180 grams
Raspberries, fresh	130 grams
Rice Bubbles	35 grams
Rice flour	200 grams
Rolled oats	90 grams
Semolina	180 grams
Sour cream	240 grams
Sugar, brown, firmly packed	220 grams
Sugar, caster	220 grams
Sugar, Demerara	220 grams
Sugar, icing sugar	160 grams
Sugar, raw	220 grams
Sugar, white	220 grams
Sultanas	160 grams
Sunflower seeds	150 grams
Walnuts	100 grams
Yoghurt, coconut	250 grams
Yoghurt, natural	260 grams

INGREDIENTS

Almond Meal is typically made by grinding blanched almonds. Some varieties available are made from whole almonds so they also contain the skins. Either variety will work in recipes. To make almond meal in the TM, place 250g of almonds into the bowl. Mill for 5 to 10 seconds on Speed 7. Sift the mixture to remove any large chunks.

Aquafaba is the starchy water legumes have been soaked and cooked it. This viscous liquid whips, binds and adds moisture making it a good substitute for eggs in vegan or egg-free baking. The most reliable aquafaba is from canned chickpeas. Simply strain a can of chickpeas over a bowl to collect the aquafaba. Any unused aquafaba can be stored in the refrigerator for up to a week or frozen.

Baking powder and Bicarbonate of Soda are both raising agents however they are not interchangeable as they create different tastes, textures and appearances in baked goods. Bicarbonate of soda can be referred to as baking soda. It is a pure raising agent that needs to be moistened and mixed with an acidic ingredient such as lemon juice or buttermilk to be activated. Baking powder is a mixture of bicarbonate of soda and an acidic ingredient such as cream of tartar. As it already acidic, it only needs to be moistened to be activated.

Butter
Recipes use salted butter at room temperature for conventional methods and cold butter for Thermomix methods unless otherwise specified. Some recipes require cold, very well softened or melted butter for both conventional and Thermomix methods as stipulated in the ingredients list. Very well softened butter should not give any resistance when pushed so that it mixes easily with other ingredients. Cut butter into 3cm cubes before using.

Vegan Butter is a substitute for butter made without animal products. Recipes have been tested using Nuttelex Buttery.

Buttermilk has a tangy taste and is acidic in nature. It adds lightness and tenderness to baked goods when it reacts with
bi-carbonate of soda.
If necessary, make a substitute for buttermilk by mixing 1 tablespoon of lemon juice or white vinegar with 1 cup of milk. Allow the mixture to stand for 5 to 10 minutes before using. Alternatively, mix 180ml of natural yoghurt with 60ml of milk.

Chocolate varies greatly in flavour so it is worthwhile buying good quality chocolate that is enjoyable to eat. Dark chocolate which contains 70% cocoa solids should be suitable for vegan diets however it is important to check the label for allergens if catering to vegan or gluten-free diets. Nestle dark, white and milk choc bits are gluten-free and Absolute Organic and Sweet William both produce chocolate chips that are vegan and gluten-free.

Cocoa used in recipes is 100% Dutch processed cocoa.

Condensed Milk is reduced and sweetened milk sold in cans with the UHT milk in supermarkets.

Condensed Coconut Milk is made from coconut milk which means it is vegan friendly. It can found it in the Asian section in the supermarket.

Cream

Double Cream is very thick due to its high fat percentage. It is ideal for dolloping and serving with baked goods.

Pure Cream is a natural cream which can be referred to as single cream or pouring cream due to its consistency. It is often used to make desserts and sauces.

Coconut Cream is a thick and rich cream made from coconut flesh and water making it suitable for vegan diets. It is sold in cans in the Asian section of the supermarket.

Sour Cream is cream which has been fermented making it thick and acidic. A good alternative is a thick, natural yoghurt.

Thickened Cream is very versatile and is the most commonly used form of cream in these recipes. It contains gelatine or a thickening agent which makes it thicker than pure cream. It is ideal for whipping however be sure not to choose light varieties for this purpose as they do not thicken and hold their shape.

Cream of Tartar is a white, acidic powder that activates bicarbonate of soda, stabilises egg whites and prevents sugar from crystallising. Use it to create fluffy cakes, chewy biscuits and stable meringue. It can be found in the baking aisle.

Custard Powder is a powdered mix used to make custard. The ingredients vary between brands so it's important to check the label for allergens if catering to gluten-free or vegan diets.

Eggs used in recipes are extra large eggs with an average weight of 58g. Choose free range eggs and allow them to come to room temperature before using.

Flours

There are so many types of flour available today, each with different characteristics and uses.

Bakers Flour is higher in protein than standard plain flour and is used for making bread. When water is added, the protein develops into glutinous strands which make dough elastic. Bakers flour is important in developing the structure and texture of bread and shouldn't be substituted.

Besan Flour may be referred to as chickpea or garbanzo flour as it is made by grinding dried chickpeas. It is a gluten-free flour alternative that helps to bind but also make baked goods light and fluffy.

Buckwheat Flour is actually made from a fruit and not a cereal as the name suggests meaning it is gluten-free. Buckwheat adds a rich, nutty flavour to baked goods with the additional health benefits of being high in fibre, protein and vitamins.

Cornflour is the finely ground starch from maize or sometimes wheat. It is used to thicken or to add softness to baked goods. Recipes in this book use cornflour made from maize which is gluten-free.

Gluten-Free Flour is a premixed blend of various gluten-free flours and starches. The particular combination and ratio of flours used differs between brands. The brand you choose will affect the end baked goods. All recipes in the book have been tested using White Wings Gluten-free plain and self-raising flours. I chose this brand as it is readily available in the baking aisle at supermarkets and is designed to bake like regular flour.

Glutinous Rice Flour is made by finely grinding sweet white rice. The name refers to the sticky, gluey consistency of the flour when it is cooked. It doesn't contain any gluten but helps to thicken, bind and give gluten-free foods a chewy texture.

Plain Flour is a general purpose flour that does not contain raising agents.

Rice Flour is finely milled rice which means it is gluten-free. It is used in cooking to give foods a crunchy texture.

Self-Raising Flour is plain flour with added raising agents. To replicate self-raising flour, add 2 teaspoons of baking powder to 1 cup (150g) of plain flour then sift together several times.

Semolina is a course flour made from durum wheat. Use it to line trays when baking bread or pizza to prevent them from sticking and produce a crunchy base.

Spelt Flour comes in both wholemeal and white varieties and has a nutty, slightly sweet flavour. It is wheat free but contains gluten. Spelt flour can be substituted with plain flour without significantly altering the texture of the baked goods.

Tapioca Flour is a gluten-free starch extracted from the cassava root. It has a mild taste and helps to thicken, bind, add moisture and a chewy texture to baked goods.

Wholemeal Flour or whole-wheat flour is made by grinding the whole wheat grain. It therefore has a nutty flavour and is more nutritious than white flour. It cannot be used interchangeably with white flour without changing the appearance, taste and texture of baked goods.

Flaxseed Meal refers to finely ground flaxseeds. It can be bought pre-milled or you can grind flaxseeds to make your own. Flaxseed meal offers a range of nutritional benefits and can be mixed with water to add structure and moisture when baking. It can be found in the health food aisle in the supermarket.

Gelatine is a setting agent that turns liquids to gel. It can be bought in sheet or powder form however recipes in this book use gelatine powder. Gelatine is made from animal products so it is not suitable for vegan diets.

Ginger

Glacè ginger is made by cooking and steeping ginger in a sugar syrup until it is soft, sweet and translucent. Naked ginger is not as soft or sweet as glacè ginger but it can be used as a substitute in the recipes.

Ground ginger is powdered, dried ginger which adds warmth and spice to baked goods.

Jel-it-in is a vegan alternative to gelatine. It has to be heated to be activated but then sets quickly. It is available in the baking aisle in the supermarket.

Marie Biscuits are plain, sweet biscuits made by Arnott's. They can be substituted with a similar type of biscuit. For vegan baking use Arnott's Nice biscuits and for gluten-free baking I like to use Coles gluten-free shortbread.

Mild Olive Oil is used in recipes as it has a delicate flavour. It can be substituted with vegetable oil if desired.

Milk in recipes refers to full cream cow's milk.

Soy milk is a dairy-free alternative to cow's milk made from soy beans. Vegan recipes use soy milk rather than other non-dairy milks because its consistency and protein content is similar to cow's milk so it produces the best results in baking.

Nutritional Yeast Flakes or savoury yeast flakes are toasted, inactive yeast flakes. They add a savoury cheese flavour in vegan baking as a substitute for Parmesan cheese.

Passionfruit can be fresh or tinned however I recommend using fresh passionfruit when they are in season because they are far more vibrant and flavoursome. The amount of pulp varies greatly between each fruit. To quickly separate juice from the seeds, scoop pulp into a bowl, whisk vigorously, (TM 30 seconds/ Reverse/Speed 4) then strain through a sieve.

Polenta as an ingredient refers to dried and ground yellow corn. Recipes use instant polenta which is quicker to cook.

Psyllium Husk is made from the husks of the Plantago ovata plant's seeds. It is high in soluble fibre and forms a gel when mixed with liquids. It is useful in gluten-free and vegan baking as it binds and provides moisture in the absence of gluten or eggs. It can be found in the health food aisle in supermarkets.

Rice Malt Syrup

Rice malt syrup is fructose free and is suitable for vegans. Rice malt syrup and honey can be used interchangeably in recipes without altering the texture however products made with honey will be far sweeter than those made with rice malt syrup.

Sugars

Brown Sugar contains molasses which gives it a moist texture and a rich taste, adding softness and a caramel flavour to baked goods. Brown sugar can be used in place of dark brown sugar however the colour and flavour will not be as intense. Measurements given for brown sugar are firmly packed.

Caster Sugar is finely granulated white sugar which is useful in baking as it dissolves easily. It can be made in the TM by milling 250g of white sugar for 2 seconds on Speed 9.

Icing Sugar Mixture is pure icing sugar with a small amount of cornflour added to prevent it from hardening. It is ideal for dusting over baked goods and making smooth, soft set icings such as buttercream. It is referred to in recipes as icing sugar.

Pure Icing Sugar is white sugar which has been milled to an ultra fine powder. It hardens with age so it needs to be sifted before use. It is ideal for making hard set icings such as royal icing. In the TM, mill 250g of white sugar for 1 minute on Speed 9. Allow to cool then repeat twice.

Raw Caster Sugar can be referred to as golden caster sugar. It maintains the flavour and colour of raw sugar but is finer in texture so it dissolves more easily. It can be made in the TM by milling 250g of raw sugar for 2 seconds on Speed 9.

Raw Sugar is golden brown in colour and has a slight honey flavour. Its course grain means it doesn't melt or dissolve easily. Sprinkle it over pies, muffins and biscuits before baking for a crunchy topping.

White Sugar is refined to leave white, medium sized granules. It is the most common form of sugar and is referred to in recipes simply as 'sugar'.

Vanilla

Vanilla Bean Paste is quick and easy to use and has a strong vanilla flavour. It works well in cakes or baked products where a pronounced vanilla flavour is desired however the seeds will be visible as little black flecks.

Vanilla Extract is mild in flavour in comparison to vanilla bean paste. The benefits are that it is economical and it is invisible as it doesn't contain the seeds. Use vanilla extract to enhance other flavours in baked goods.

Yeast

There are two forms of yeast readily available in supermarkets; instant dried yeast and active dry yeast. The type of yeast used in recipes is determined by the desired characteristics of the bread. Instant dried yeast is fast acting and causes doughs to rise rapidly. It is used to create soft and fluffy loaves and buns. Active dry yeast is used to create a flavoursome loaf that results from a slow fermentation.

THERMOMIX TERMS

The recipes include both conventional and Thermomix methods. If using the Thermomix, follow the conventional method then refer to the bold type at the end of each step for specific Thermomix settings and instructions. If no Thermomix instructions are provided for a particular step, it should be completed in the conventional manner. A description of the Thermomix terms and instructions used throughout the book are outlined below.

TM - Thermomix
TM indicates that an instruction is specific to Thermomix users.

TTS - Time/Temperature/Speed
The settings are written in the order of Time/Temperature/Speed as this is the order in which they should be programmed.

Butterfly - Insert Whisk Attachment
Insert the butterfly before adding ingredients into the TM bowl. The butterfly locks into place between the blunt side of the upper blades and the sharp side of the lower blades.

Varoma
Set temperature to Varoma, which is the highest heat setting available on non-programmed recipes.

Soft Stir
Set TM to soft stir which is the slowest speed setting. Turn speed dial to soft stir as indicated by the spoon encompassed by a circle to gently stir mixtures.

Turbo
Set the TM to Turbo mode which is the highest speed used to quickly chop hard foods using a pulsing motion. The turbo setting will not operate if the temperature is above 60°C.

Knead - Wheat Symbol
Set the TM to dough mode. In TM31, turn the speed dial to closed lid then press the wheat symbol. In the TM5, press the wheat symbol then select dough. For the TM6, select dough mode then set the desired time. The TM moves around on the bench top when kneading so do not leave it unattended.

Reverse
Set the TM blades to reverse to fold through ingredients without chopping them. Reverse is indicated by a circular reverse arrow.

Set Aside
Remove the ingredients after the step is complete and set aside until needed. Wash and dry the TM bowl if necessary.

MC Off - Measuring Cup Off
Leave the measuring cup off when the TM is whisking using the butterfly attachment or reducing on the Varoma setting. The simmering basket or splash guard can be placed on the lid when the measuring cup is off to prevent mixtures from splattering.

Add Gradually
Add the ingredients gradually through the measuring cup hole in the lid whilst the TM is in operation.

Scrape Halfway
Halfway through the step, pause the TM, remove the lid then use a flexible spatula to scrape down the mixture from the sides of the bowl, the lid and from under the blades.

Scrape
Scrape down the sides of the bowl and under the blades at the end of the step. Whilst it is not stated at the end of each particular step, it is beneficial to do this before moving onto the next step.

Assist with Spatula
Insert the TM spatula in the MC hole and use it to help move the ingredients around the bowl whilst the TM is in operation. The TM spatula has a special safety shield which prevents it from connecting with the blades. No other implements should be used in the TM whilst the motor is on.

HANDY TIPS FOR BAKING WITH THE THERMOMIX

Prepare ingredients
Check the ingredients list to see if any ingredients need to prepared before proceeding with the recipe. Prepare dry ingredients first then wet ingredients to avoid having to wash the bowl in between.

Weigh
Check the scales are weighing accurately before beginning a recipe by testing something with a known weight. Ingredients can be weighed directly into the TM bowl or into a bowl placed on the TM lid. Reset the scales to zero between each ingredient.

Cream
Creaming in the TM is best achieved by beating cold butter with sugar on low speeds for longer periods of time. Beat the butter and sugar on Speed 3 until well combined then increase to Speed 4 until pale and fluffy.

Mix
Don't mix cake batters too vigorously. Use Speed 3 when mixing small amounts or thin batters or Speed 4 for thicker batters or larger amounts.

Whip
Whipping requires the butterfly to be inserted. For optimal aeration, set the TM to Speed 3 and leave the MC off. Do not exceed Speed 4 otherwise the butterfly can become dislodged.

Heat, Cook, Melt, Sauté & Reduce
The TM will not heat unless a time has been set. Cut ingredients into even pieces and use a low speed so they don't splatter. Sauté and reduce mixtures on temperatures from 100°C to Varoma. Leave the MC off to allow steam to escape and place the simmering basket or splash guard on the lid.

Knead
For soft and fluffy bread, knead dough for 8 minutes until smooth and elastic. Keep kneading time under a minute when making scone, biscuit and pastry doughs to avoid activating the gluten and making them tough.

Chop
Ingredients prepared in the TM will not be as uniformly chopped as those cut by hand. For the most consistent results, cut foods into even sized pieces and only half fill the bowl. To prevent sticky foods like dried apricots from clumping together, add a teaspoon of icing sugar or flour. Chop in 2 second intervals using Speed 4 for softer ingredients and Speed 5 for firmer ingredients. Turn the speed dial quickly to the desired speed unless ingredients are hot.

Sift
Sift dry ingredients together for 10 seconds on Speed 5.

Blend
Blend wet mixtures on Speed 6 and increase the speed to 9 if the mixture includes hard ingredients. Always turn the speed up gradually when blending, particularly if the mixture is hot.

Grate
Foods grate best when they are firm so partially freeze them if necessary. Cut or break foods into 3cm pieces and process in 200g batches. Grate semi-hard ingredients like tasty cheese on Speed 7 and hard foods such as Parmesan on Speed 9. Process for 5 to 10 seconds depending on the desired consistency.

Zest
Peel the skin from the fruit in long strips, avoiding the white pith. Process on Speed 9, scraping down the sides of the bowl at 10 second intervals.

Mill
Ensure the TM bowl, blades and lid are completely dry then mill in 100g to 250g batches. Mill nuts on Speed 7 for 5 to 10 seconds but avoid over processing or they will become a paste.
When finely milling grains and sugar, place a tea towel over the lid and allow time for the mixture to settle before removing the lid. Set the TM to Speed 9 and mill for up to a minute at a time. Sift mixtures to ensure no large particles remain.

TIPS FOR VEGAN BAKING

What is vegan food?
Vegan foods do not contain any products that come from animals. This excludes meat, eggs, dairy foods such as butter, milk and cheese as well as products like honey and gelatine from vegan diets.

Why do people follow a vegan diet?
People may follow a vegan diet because of personal beliefs or because of an intolerance to animal proteins. Eggs and dairy are common allergens.

Labels are important
Read the labels of all of the ingredients. Some foods are obviously not vegan friendly but animal products can also be used inconspicuously in the production of many foods like jelly, chocolate, soy cheese and beer. Check the allergen warnings and ingredients list carefully before using.

There's no one solution
Different combinations of ingredients are needed to create the right flavour and texture. Eggs play a number of roles in baking including lifting, binding and adding moisture and flavour and different substitutes will be needed to perform these functions.

Follow instructions
If you're new to vegan baking, start with an easy recipe like muffins that only require minor changes. Follow the recipes carefully and avoid improvising as particular ingredients and quantities are needed to make the recipes successful.

Show favouritism
Find your favourite brands for different ingredients then stick with them so you can achieve consistent results. A few of my favourite vegan friendly ingredients are Nuttelex Buttery, Vitasoy Soy Milky Regular, Cocobella Natural Coconut Yoghurt and Edgell canned chickpeas for aquafaba.

Look for recipes labelled V or VA.
V vegan friendly recipe
VA vegan alteration provided

TIPS FOR SUCCESSFUL GLUTEN-FREE BAKING

What is Gluten?
Gluten is the collective name for proteins found in varieties of wheat, spelt, rye, barley and triticale. When hydrated, gluten forms a sticky network which provides foods with structure and texture.

Why avoid gluten?
Coeliac disease is an autoimmune condition whereby gluten triggers gastrointestinal symptoms and causes damage to the small intestine. A strict gluten-free diet is essential in managing the disease. Many other people choose to follow a gluten-free diet because they experience similar adverse symptoms when they ingest gluten.

Labels are important
It is important to read the labels of all of the ingredients when baking for people who follow a gluten-free diet. Some foods obviously need to be avoided because they contain gluten including flour, malt, bread, pastry and biscuits however gluten may also be present in many inconspicuous foods such as soy milk, chocolate, rice malt syrup, sprinkles and baking powder. Look for foods marked with a gluten-free label otherwise read the allergen warnings and ingredients list carefully before using.

Weigh it up
1 cup of gluten-free flour does not weigh the same as a cup of regular flour so use scales rather than measuring cups to measure out ingredients.

Choose quality
The particular combination and ratio of flours used in gluten-free flour mixes differs between brands and this will affect the end baked goods. Choose a reputable brand and when you have found one that you like, stick with it so you can achieve consistent results. All recipes in the book have been tested using White Wings Gluten-free plain and self-raising flours because they are readily available in the baking aisle at supermarkets and are designed to bake like regular flour.

There's no one solution
Substituting regular flour with gluten-free flour won't work for all recipes. Often you need to use a combination of flours or ingredients to replicate the flavour, texture, moisture and structure that gluten provides.

Ramp up the flavour
Some gluten-free flours tend to lack flavour whilst others have strong flavours. Balance them out by adding a little extra vanilla, spice or zest.

Follow instructions
If you're new to gluten-free baking, follow the recipes carefully and avoid improvising. Only begin to experiment once you are comfortable with the basics.

Whisk away
Many gluten-free recipes use a combination of flours. Sift or whisk them together before adding them to ensure they are well mixed.

Watch the clock
Gluten provides moisture and helps to bind. Watch the cooking time because gluten-free goods will bake quicker and will be dry and crumbly if they are overcooked.

Clean up
Even trace amounts of gluten can trigger reactions or damage so make sure your work space and equipment is cleaned properly and free from gluten.

Look for recipes labelled GF or GFA.
GF gluten-free recipe
GFA gluten-free alteration provided

INDEX

BAKE & ENJOY

Rachel Gray

ISBN: 9780909608798		Qty
RRP	AU$34.99	.....
Postage within Australia	AU$5.00	.....
	TOTAL* $________	

* All prices include GST

Name: ....

Address: ....

....

Phone: ....

Email: ....

Payment: [ ] Money Order [ ] Cheque [ ] MasterCard [ ] Visa

Cardholder's Name: ....

Credit Card Number: ....

Signature:..

Expiry Date: ....

Allow 7 days for delivery.

Payment to: Marzocco Consultancy (ABN 14 067 257 390)
PO Box 452
Torquay Victoria 3228
Australia

Be Published

Publish through a successful publisher.

Brolga Publishing is represented through:

- National book trade distribution, including sales, marketing & distribution through Simon & Schuster.
- International book trade distribution to:
  - The United Kingdom
  - North America
  - Sales representation in South East Asia
- Worldwide e-Book distribution